The New Faber Book of Children's Poems

The New Faber Book
of Children's Poems

edited by MATTHEW SWEENEY

with illustrations by
SARA FANELLI

ff

faber and faber

First published in 2001
by Faber and Faber Limited
3 Queen Square London WC1N 3AU
This paperback edition first published in 2003

Photoset by Wilmaset Ltd, Birkenhead, Wirral
Printed and bound in Great Britain by
Mackays of Chatham plc, Chatham, Kent

Introduction and this selection © Matthew Sweeney, 2001
Illustrations © Sara Fanelli, 2001

The right of Matthew Sweeney to be identified as editor
of this work has been asserted in accordance with Section 77
of the Copyright, Designs and Patents Act 1988

A CIP record for this book
is available from the British Library

ISBN 0–571–21905–5

10 9 8 7 6 5 4 3 2 1

Contents

Introduction

In Australia in early 2000 I mentioned to a poet that I was editing this anthology. He wished me good luck, saying it would have to be good to follow Janet Adam Smith's hallmark 1953 anthology, *The Faber Book of Children's Verse*. I agreed with him that that book casts a daunting shadow. Initially, in my own head, I'd been unsure about whether or not I was supposed to produce an updated edition of the existing book, but the more I thought about it, the less attractive that course began to seem. Whatever I came up with would be a dilution of the original, if not an effrontery. I quickly came to realise that I had to compile my own anthology from scratch, using the excellence of the 1953 book as a spur.

Besides, the lie of the land is a bit different these days. Since 1953 there has been a phenomenal growth in poetry written for children, and this would have to be adequately represented. Finding a way of balancing children's poems with whatever classic poems I might want to include would be a delicate business. But, as Auden said, 'While there are some good poems which are only for adults, because they presuppose adult experience in their readers, there are no good poems which are only for children.' And Charles Causley, in a Radio 4 interview some years back, said: 'A children's poem is simply one which a child can comprehend as well as an adult. It has to be a poem, not a jingle, not a silly collection of rhymes – a real poem.' One way of looking at it is that a good children's poem is two poems simultaneously – one for children, one for adults. And what children's poetry has in abundance is a playfulness and inventiveness, and is perhaps necessarily colloquially rooted – all of these being qualities I like in poetry.

In a way, children are the ideal readers of poetry. If a poem is about questions rather than answers, and the reader of a poem has to use his or her imagination to fill out the story – or, as it were, finish the writing of the poem, as a teenager in Guernsey put it to me once – what better readers than children, whose imaginations are so vibrant and unforced?

As I began to gather poems, I decided to admit a third category – poems written for adults that I felt would speak to children. These, I hoped, would have a second life (perhaps unintended) for children. They also helped me gauge the quality of the children's poems I laid alongside them. Shortcomings in craft or technique were quickly highlighted by this exercise in comparison, and many children's poems didn't make the final selection as a consequence. Another result of this was the exclusion of any children's poetry that was pitched too young. So I see this anthology as being aimed at older primary school children and the early teens – 9 to 15, say – although I would hope it would appeal to adult lovers of poetry as well.

If the selection is seen as cheeky, this is intended. There are a lot of anthologies for children, and too many of them show obvious signs of crossbreeding with other anthologies. I determined that this one would be different, and would have – amid the familiar, indispensable pieces – poems that no one would be expecting, or that were rarely, if ever, seen in children's anthologies. I also decided that big subjects like death would be well represented. In this I was following my predecessor, who in her introduction to the 1953 anthology wrote: 'I have no patience with those who say that love and death are not proper subjects for children. Children can often respond to these large subjects with minds less coarsened and imaginations less infected than their print-sodden elders.'

One main area in which I have deviated from the earlier book is my decision not to group the poems in sections. Instead, I've tried to arrange them in an order where light might be thrown on the poems by how they interact with or glint off their neighbours. In this I allowed myself to be led by instinct, with a certain playfulness sometimes in evidence, although my intention was always serious.

And finally, I'd like to hope that these poems will be read aloud, as well as read quietly on the page, as I believe strongly that a poem lives both in the visual and the oral/aural sphere – or as my friend the poet Thomas Lynch puts it: 'Before it is a written and read thing, it is a heard and a said thing.' Maybe this order of things explains why there are people who like to listen to poetry read aloud but who would never open a poetry book. And reading a poem aloud can make it attractive to very young readers, even if it's simply the noise of the poem they are drawn to. Noise is something a poem excels in. It would be a shame not to bring this out.

Manners

For a Child of 1918

My grandfather said to me
as we sat on the wagon seat,
'Be sure to remember to always
speak to everyone you meet.'

We met a stranger on foot.
My grandfather's whip tapped his hat.
'Good day, sir. Good day. A fine day.'
And I said it and bowed where I sat.

Then we overtook a boy we knew
with his big pet crow on his shoulder.
'Always offer everyone a ride;
don't forget that when you get older,'

my grandfather said. So Willy
climbed up with us, but the crow
gave a 'Caw!' and flew off. I was worried.
How would he know where to go?

But he flew a little way at a time
from fence post to fence post, ahead;
and when Willy whistled he answered.
'A fine bird,' my grandfather said,

'and he's well brought up. See, he answers
nicely when he's spoken to.
Man or beast, that's good manners.
Be sure that you both always do.'

When automobiles went by,
the dust hid the people's faces,

but we shouted 'Good day! Good day!
Fine day!' at the top of our voices.

When we came to Hustler Hill,
he said that the mare was tired,
so we all got down and walked,
as our good manners required.

ELIZABETH BISHOP

Monkeys

Two little creatures
With faces the size of
A pair of pennies
Are clasping each other.
'Ah, do not leave me,'
One says to the other,
In the high monkey-
Cage in the beast-shop.

There are no people
To gape at them now,
For people are loth to
Peer in the dimness;
Have they not builded
Streets and playhouses,
Sky-signs and bars,
To lose the loneliness
Shaking the hearts
Of the two little Monkeys?

Yes. But who watches
The penny-small faces

Can hear the voices:
'Ah, do not leave me;
Suck I will give you,
Warmth and clasping,
And if you slip from
This beam I can never
Find you again.'

Dim is the evening,
And chill is the weather;
There, drawn from their coloured
Hemisphere,
The apes lilliputian
With faces the size of
A pair of pennies,
And voices as low as
The flow of my blood.

PADRAIC COLUM

Child on Top of a Greenhouse

The wind billowing out the seat of my britches,
My feet crackling splinters of glass and dried putty,
The half grown chrysanthemums staring up like accusers,
Up through the streaked glass, flashing with sunlight,
A few white clouds all rushing eastward,
A line of elms plunging and tossing like horses,
And everyone, everyone pointing up and shouting!

THEODORE ROETHKE

[3]

Allie

Allie, call the birds in,
  The birds from the sky!
Allie calls, Allie sings,
  Down they all fly:
First there came
Two white doves,
  Then a sparrow from his nest,
Then a clucking bantam hen,
  Then a robin red-breast.

Allie, call the beasts in,
  The beasts, every one!
Allie calls, Allie sings,
  In they all run:
First there came
Two black lambs,
  Then a grunting Berkshire sow,
Then a dog without a tail,
  Then a red and white cow.

Allie, call the fish up,
  The fish from the stream!
Allie calls, Allie sings,
  Up they all swim:
First there came
Two gold fish,
  A minnow and a miller's thumb,
Then a school of little trout,
  Then the twisting eels come.

Allie, call the children,
  Call them from the green!

Allie calls, Allie sings,
    Soon they run in:
First there came
Tom and Madge,
    Kate and I who'll not forget
How we played by the water's edge
    Till the April sun set.

ROBERT GRAVES

Thrum Drew a Small Map

Thrum drew
A small map

He put in
The small countries
The lizards and
The bugs and
The snails and
The worms

He made a mountain
And a green tree
And small rocks
And smaller rocks

He made a river
And a little fish

He made a meadow
And a little house

He made specks
That were ants
He made a queer smile
On the countenance of
A bee

He made a person
Small as a
Minnow

He made white birds
In a blue sky
But because he had no
Yellow
He couldn't draw the sun

He made an ocean
And a small boat

He made daytime and
Nighttime and a
Small evening star

He signed his name
In small letters
At the bottom
Almost too small
To be able to
See

He loved his small
Map
With its small
Small secrets

Grim came and tore it
Up

SUSAN MUSGRAVE

THRUM

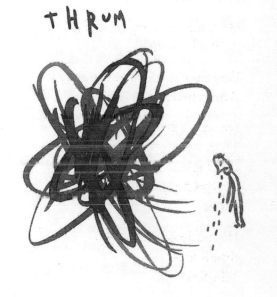

Following a Lark

A Country Boy Goes to School

   I

There he is, first lark this year
   Loud, between
That raincloud and the sun, lost
Up there, a long sky run, what peltings of song!
   (Six times 6, 36. Six times 7, 42
   Six times eight is . . .)
Oh, Mr Ferguson, have mercy at arithmetic time
   On peedie Tom o' the Glebe.

   2

There's Gyre's ewe has 2 lambs.
   Snow on the ridge still.
How many more days do I have to take
This peat under my oxter
   For the school fire?
(James the Sixth, Charles the First . . . Who then?)
Oh, Mr Ferguson, I swear
   I knew all the Stewarts last night.

   3

Yes, Mistress Wylie, we're all fine.
   A pandrop! Oh, thank you.
I must hurry, Mistress Wylie,
   Old Ferguson
Gets right mad if a boy's late.
I was late twice last week.
   Do you know this, Mistress Wylie,

The capital of Finland is Helsingfors . . .
   Yes, I'll tell Grannie
You have four fat geese this summer.

   4

When I get to the top of the brae
I'll see the kirk, the school, the shop,
   Smithy and inn and boatyard.
I wish I was that tinker boy
Going on over the hill, the wind in his rags.

Look, the schoolyard's like a throng of bees.

   5

I wish Willie Thomson
   Would take me on his creel-boat!
'Tom, there's been six generations of Corstons
   Working the Glebe,
And I doubt there'll never be fish-scales
On your hands, or salt in your boots . . .'

(Sixteen ounces, one pound. Fourteen pounds, one stone.)
A sack of corn's a hundredweight.
   I think a whale must be bigger than a ton.

   6

Jimmo Spence, he told me
   Where the lark's nest is.
   Beside a stone in his father's oatfield,
   The high granite corner.

('I wandered lonely as a cloud . . .' Oh where? What then?)

I could go up by the sheep track
    Now the scholars are in their pen
And *Scallop* and *Mayflower* are taking the flood
    And the woman of Fea
Is pinning her washing to the wind.

I could wait for the flutter of the lark coming down.

7

The school bell! Oh, my heart's
Pounding louder than any bell.

    A quarter of a mile to run.
    My bare feet
    Have broken three daffodils in the field.

Heart thunderings, last tremor of the bell
    And the lark wing-folded.

'Late again, Master Thomas Corston of Glebe farm.
Enter, sir. With the greatest interest
    We all await your explanation
Of a third morning's dereliction.'

GEORGE MACKAY BROWN

'A narrow Fellow in the Grass'

A narrow Fellow in the Grass
Occasionally rides –
You may have met Him – did you not
His notice sudden is –

The Grass divides as with a Comb –
A spotted shaft is seen –
And then it closes at your feet
And opens further on –

He likes a Boggy Acre
A Floor too cool for Corn –
Yet when a Boy, and Barefoot –
I more than once at Noon
Have passed, I thought, a Whip lash
Unbraiding in the Sun
When stooping to secure it
It wrinkled, and was gone –

Several of Nature's People
I know, and they know me –
I feel for them a transport
Of cordiality –

But never met this Fellow
Attended, or alone
Without a tighter breathing
And Zero at the Bone –

EMILY DICKINSON

The Fly

She sat on a willow-trunk
watching
part of the battle of Crécy,
the shouts,
the gasps,

the groans,
the tramping and the tumbling.

During the fourteenth charge
of the French cavalry
she mated
with a brown-eyed male fly
from Vadincourt.

She rubbed her legs together
as she sat on a disembowelled horse
meditating
on the immortality of flies.

With relief she alighted
on the blue tongue
of the Duke of Clervaux.

When silence settled
and only the whisper of decay
softly circled the bodies

and only
a few arms and legs
still twitched jerkily under the trees,

she began to lay her eggs
on the single eye
of Johann Uhr,
the Royal Armourer.

And thus it was
that she was eaten by a swift
fleeing
from the fires of Estrées.

MIROSLAV HOLUB
(*translated by George Theiner and Ian Milner*)

[12]

Oranges and Lemons

Oranges and lemons,
Say the bells of St Clement's.

You owe me five farthings,
Say the bells of St Martin's.

When will you pay me?
Say the bells of Old Bailey.

When I grow rich,
Say the bells of Shoreditch.

When will that be?
Say the bells of Stepney.

I'm sure I don't know,
Says the great bell at Bow.

Here comes a candle to light you to bed,
Here comes a chopper to chop off your head.

ANONYMOUS

Little Fan

'I don't like the look of little Fan, mother,
    I don't like her looks a little bit.
Her face – well, it's not exactly different,
    But there's something wrong with it.

'She went down to the sea-shore yesterday,
    And she talked to somebody there,
Now she won't do anything but sit
    And comb out her yellowy hair.

'Her eyes are shiny and she sings, mother,
    Like nobody ever sang before.
Perhaps they gave her something queer to eat,
    Down by the rocks on the shore.

'Speak to me, speak, little Fan dear,
    Aren't you feeling very well?
Where have you been and what are you singing,
    And what's that seaweedy smell?

'Where did you get that shiny comb, love,
    And those pretty coral beads so red?
Yesterday you had two legs, I'm certain,
    But now there's something else instead.

'I don't like the looks of little Fan, mother,
    You'd best go and close the door.
Watch now, or she'll be gone for ever
    To the rocks by the brown sandy shore.'

JAMES REEVES

A Case of Murder

They should not have left him there alone,
Alone that is except for the cat.
He was only nine, not old enough
To be left alone in a basement flat,
Alone, that is, except for the cat.
A dog would have been a different thing,
A big gruff dog with slashing jaws,
But a cat with round eyes mad as gold,
Plump as a cushion with tucked-in paws –
Better have left him with a fair-sized rat!

But what they did was leave him with a cat.
He hated that cat; he watched it sit,
A buzzing machine of soft black stuff,
He sat and watched and he hated it,
Snug in its fur, hot blood in a muff,
And its mad gold stare and the way it sat
Crooning dark warmth: he loathed all that.
So he took Daddy's stick and he hit the cat.
Then quick as a sudden crack in a glass
It hissed, black flash, to a hiding place
In the dust and dark beneath the couch,
And he followed the grin on his new-made face,
A wide-eyed, frightened snarl of a grin,
And he took the stick and he thrust it in,
Hard and quick in the furry dark,
The black fur squealed and he felt his skin
Prickle with sparks of dry delight.
Then the cat again came into sight,
Shot for the door that wasn't quite shut,
But the boy, quick too, slammed fast the door:
The cat, half-through, was cracked like a nut
And the soft black thud was dumped on the floor.
Then the boy was suddenly terrified
And he bit his knuckles and cried and cried;
But he had to do something with the dead thing there.
His eyes squeezed beads of salty prayer
But the wound of fear gaped wide and raw;
He dared not touch the thing with his hands
So he fetched a spade and shovelled it
And dumped the load of heavy fur
In the spidery cupboard under the stair
Where it's been for years, and though it died
It's grown in that cupboard and its hot low purr

Grows slowly louder year by year:
There'll not be a corner for the boy to hide
When the cupboard swells and all sides split
And the huge black cat pads out of it.

VERNON SCANNELL

Don't-Care

Don't-Care – he didn't care,
   Don't-Care was wild:
Don't-Care stole plum and pear
   Like any beggar's child.

Don't-Care was made to care,
   Don't-Care was hung:
Don't-Care was put in a pot
   And stewed till he was done.

ANONYMOUS

The Dumb Soldier

When the grass was closely mown,
Walking on the lawn alone,
In the turf a hole I found
And hid a soldier underground.

Spring and daisies came apace;
Grasses hide my hiding place;
Grasses run like a green sea
O'er the lawn up to my knee.

Under grass alone he lies,
Looking up with leaden eyes,
Scarlet coat and pointed gun,
To the stars and to the sun.

When the grass is ripe like grain,
When the scythe is stoned again,
When the lawn is shaven clear,
Then my hole shall reappear.

I shall find him, never fear,
I shall find my grenadier;
But for all that's gone and come,
I shall find my soldier dumb.

He has lived, a little thing,
In the grassy woods of spring;
Done, if he could tell me true,
Just as I should like to do.

He has seen the starry hours
And the springing of the flowers;
And the fairy things that pass
In the forests of the grass.

In the silence he has heard
Talking bee and ladybird,
And the butterfly has flown
O'er him as he lay alone.

Not a word will he disclose,
Not a word of all he knows.
I must lay him on the shelf,
And make up the tale myself.

ROBERT LOUIS STEVENSON

True Story

This morning I jumped on my horse
And went out for a ride,
And some wild outlaws chased me
And they shot me in the side.
So I crawled into a wildcat's cave
To find a place to hide,
But some pirates found me sleeping there,
And soon they had me tied
To a pole and built a fire
Under me – I almost cried
Till a mermaid came and cut me loose
And begged to be my bride,
So I said I'd come back Wednesday
But I must admit I lied.
Then I ran into a jungle swamp
But I forgot my guide
And I stepped into some quicksand,
And no matter how I tried
I couldn't get out, until I met
A water snake named Clyde,
Who pulled me to some cannibals
Who planned to have me fried.
But an eagle came and swooped me up
And through the air we flied,
But he dropped me in a boiling lake
A thousand miles wide.
And you'll never guess what I did then –
I DIED.

SHEL SILVERSTEIN

[18]

The Sands of Dee

'O Mary, go and call the cattle home,
    And call the cattle home,
    And call the cattle home
  Across the sands of Dee;'
The western wind was wild and dank with foam,
  And all alone went she.

The western tide crept up along the sand,
    And o'er and o'er the sand,
    And round and round the sand,
  As far as eye could see.
The rolling mist came down and hid the land:
  And never home came she.

'Oh! is it weed, or fish, or floating hair –
    A tress of golden hair,
    A drownèd maiden's hair
  Above the nets at sea?
Was never salmon yet that shone so fair
  Among the stakes on Dee.'

They rowed her in across the rolling foam,
    The cruel crawling foam,
    The cruel hungry foam,
  To her grave beside the sea:
But still the boatmen hear her call the cattle home
  Across the sands of Dee.

CHARLES KINGSLEY

What Has Happened to Lulu?

What has happened to Lulu, mother?
    What has happened to Lu?
There's nothing in her bed but an old rag-doll
    And by its side a shoe.

Why is her window wide, mother,
    The curtain flapping free,
And only a circle on the dusty shelf
    Where her money-box used to be?

Why do you turn your head, mother,
    And why do the tear-drops fall?
And why do you crumple that note on the fire
    And say it is nothing at all?

I woke to voices late last night,
    I heard an engine roar.
Why do you tell me the things I heard
    Were a dream and nothing more?

I heard somebody cry, mother,
    In anger or in pain,
But now I ask you why, mother,
    You say it was a gust of rain.

Why do you wander about as though
    You don't know what to do?
What has happened to Lulu, mother?
    What has happened to Lu?

CHARLES CAUSLEY

'Who is the East?'

Who is the East?
The Yellow Man
Who may be Purple if He can
That carries in the Sun.

Who is the West?
The Purple Man
Who may be Yellow if He can
That lets Him out again.

EMILY DICKINSON

The Worms at Heaven's Gate

Out of the tomb, we bring Badroulbadour,
Within our bellies, we her chariot.
Here is an eye. And here are, one by one,
The lashes of that eye and its white lid.
Here is the cheek on which that lid declined,
And, finger after finger, here, the hand,
The genius of that cheek. Here are the lips,
The bundle of the body and the feet.

Out of the tomb we bring Badroulbadour.

WALLACE STEVENS

Beachcomber

Monday I found a boot –
Rust and salt leather.
I gave it back to the sea, to dance in.

Tuesday a spar of timber worth thirty bob.
Next winter
It will be a chair, a coffin, a bed.

Wednesday a half can of Swedish spirits.
I tilted my head.
The shore was cold with mermaids and angels.

Thursday I got nothing, seaweed,
A whale bone,
Wet feet and a bad cough.

Friday I held a seaman's skull,
Sand spilling from it
The way time is told on kirkyard stones.

Saturday a barrel of sodden oranges.
A Spanish ship
Was wrecked last month at The Kame.

Sunday, for fear of the elders,
I smoke on the stone.
What's heaven? A sea chest with a thousand gold coins.

GEORGE MACKAY BROWN

Birches

When I see birches bend to left and right
Across the lines of straighter darker trees,
I like to think some boy's been swinging them.
But swinging doesn't bend them down to stay.
Ice-storms do that. Often you must have seen them
Loaded with ice a sunny winter morning
After a rain. They click upon themselves
As the breeze rises, and turn many-colored
As the stir cracks and crazes their enamel.
Soon the sun's warmth makes them shed crystal shells
Shattering and avalanching on the snow-crust –
Such heaps of broken glass to sweep away
You'd think the inner dome of heaven had fallen.
They are dragged to the withered bracken by the load,
And they seem not to break; though once they are bowed
So low for long, they never right themselves:
You may see their trunks arching in the woods
Years afterwards, trailing their leaves on the ground
Like girls on hands and knees that throw their hair
Before them over their heads to dry in the sun.
But I was going to say when Truth broke in
With all her matter-of-fact about the ice-storm
I should prefer to have some boy bend them
As he went out and in to fetch the cows –
Some boy too far from town to learn baseball,
Whose only play was what he found himself,
Summer or winter, and could play alone.
One by one he subdued his father's trees
By riding them down over and over again
Until he took the stiffness out of them,
And not one but hung limp, not one was left

[23]

For him to conquer. He learned all there was
To learn about not launching out too soon
And so not carrying the tree away
Clear to the ground. He always kept his poise
To the top branches, climbing carefully
With the same pains you use to fill a cup

Up to the brim, and even above the brim.
Then he flung outward, feet first, with a swish,
Kicking his way down through the air to the ground.
So was I once myself a swinger of birches.
And so I dream of going back to be.
It's when I'm weary of considerations,
And life is too much like a pathless wood
Where your face burns and tickles with the cobwebs
Broken across it, and one eye is weeping
From a twig's having lashed across it open.
I'd like to get away from earth awhile
And then come back to it and begin over.
May no fate willfully misunderstand me
And half grant what I wish and snatch me away
Not to return. Earth's the right place for love:
I don't know where it's likely to go better.
I'd like to go by climbing a birch tree,
And climb black branches up a snow-white trunk
Toward heaven, till the tree could bear no more,
But dipped its top and set me down again.
That would be good both going and coming back.
One could do worse than be a swinger of birches.

ROBERT FROST

The Sea Boy

Peter went – and nobody there –
Down by the sandy sea,
And he danced a jig, while the moon shone big,
All in his lone danced he;
And the surf splashed over his tippeting toes,

And he sang his riddle-cum-ree,
With hair a-dangling,
Moon a-spangling
The bubbles and froth of the sea.
He danced him to, and he danced him fro,
And he twirled himself about,
And now the starry waves tossed in,
And now the waves washed out;
Bare as an acorn, bare as a nut,
Nose and toes and knee,
Peter the sea-boy danced and pranced,
And sang his riddle-cum-ree.

WALTER DE LA MARE

from A Christmas Childhood

My father played the melodion
Outside at our gate;
There were stars in the morning east
And they danced to his music.

Across the wild bogs his melodion called
To Lennons and Callans.
As I pulled on my trousers in a hurry
I knew some strange thing had happened.

Outside in the cow-house my mother
Made the music of milking;
The light of her stable-lamp was a star
And the frost of Bethlehem made it twinkle.

A water-hen screeched in the bog,
Mass-going feet
Crunched the wafer-ice on the pot-holes,
Somebody wistfully twisted the bellows wheel.

My child poet picked out the letters
On the grey stone,
In silver the wonder of a Christmas townland,
The winking glitter of a frosty dawn.

Cassiopeia was over
Cassidy's hanging hill,
I looked and three whin bushes rode across
The horizon – the Three Wise Kings.

An old man passing said:
'Can't he make it talk' –
The melodion. I hid in the doorway
And tightened the belt of my box-pleated coat.

I nicked six nicks on the door-post
With my penknife's big blade –
There was a little one for cutting tobacco.
And I was six Christmases of age.

My father played the melodion,
My mother milked the cows,
And I had a prayer like a white rose pinned
On the Virgin Mary's blouse.

PATRICK KAVANAGH

What Does the Clock Say?

What does the clock say?
Nothing at all.
It hangs all day
and night on the wall
with nothing to say
with nothing to tell
except sometimes
to ting a bell.
And yet it is strange
that the short and the tall
the large, the clever,
the great and the small
will do nothing whatever
nothing at all
without asking it,
the clock on the wall.

GEORGE BARKER

At a Country Fair

At a bygone Western country fair
I saw a giant led by a dwarf
With a red string like a long thin scarf;
How much he was the stronger there
  The giant seemed unaware.

And then I saw that the giant was blind,
And the dwarf a shrewd-eyed little thing;
The giant, mild, timid, obeyed the string

As if he had no independent mind,
    Or will of any kind.

Wherever the dwarf decided to go
At his heels the other trotted meekly,
(Perhaps – I know not – reproaching weakly)
Like one Fate bade that it must be so,
    Whether he wished or no.

Various sights in various climes
I have seen, and more I may see yet,
But that sight never shall I forget,
And have thought it the sorriest of pantomimes,
    If once, a hundred times!

THOMAS HARDY

'What's your name?'

What's your name?
Pudden Tame.
What's your other?
Bread and Butter.
Where do you live?
In a sieve.
What's your number?
Cucumber.

ANONYMOUS

Cottleston Pie

Cottleston, Cottleston, Cottleston Pie.
A fly can't bird, but a bird can fly.
Ask me a riddle and I reply:
'Cottleston, Cottleston, Cottleston Pie.'

Cottleston, Cottleston, Cottleston Pie.
A fish can't whistle and neither can I.
Ask me a riddle and I reply:
'Cottleston, Cottleston, Cottleston Pie.'

Cottleston, Cottleston, Cottleston Pie.
Why does a chicken, I don't know why.
Ask me a riddle and I reply:
'Cottleston, Cottleston, Cottleston Pie.'

A. A. MILNE

'The Wind'

The Wind – tapped like a tired Man –
And like a Host – 'Come in'
I boldly answered – entered then
My Residence within

A Rapid – footless Guest –
To offer whom a Chair
Were as impossible as hand
A Sofa to the Air –

No Bone had He to bind Him –
His speech was like the Push
Of numerous Humming Birds at once
From a superior Bush –

His Countenance – a Billow –
His Fingers, as He passed
Let go a music – as of tunes
Blown tremulous in Glass –

He visited – still flitting
Then like a timid Man
Again, He tapped – 'twas flurriedly –
And I became alone –

EMILY DICKINSON

John Mouldy

I spied John Mouldy in his cellar,
Deep down twenty steps of stone;
In the dusk he sat a-smiling,
    Smiling there alone.

He read no book, he snuffed no candle;
The rats ran in, the rats ran out;
And far and near, the drip of water
   Went whisp'ring about.

The dusk was still, with dew a-falling,
I saw the Dog-star bleak and grim,
I saw a slim brown rat of Norway
   Creep over him.

I spied John Mouldy in his cellar,
Deep down twenty steps of stone;
In the dusk he sat a-smiling,
   Smiling there alone.

WALTER DE LA MARE

Bog-Face

Dear little Bog-Face,
Why are you so cold?
And why do you lie with your eyes shut? –
You are not very old.

I am a Child of this World,
And a Child of Grace,
And Mother, I shall be glad when it is over,
I am Bog-Face.

STEVIE SMITH

The Fiddler of Dooney

When I play on my fiddle in Dooney,
Folk dance like a wave of the sea;
My cousin is priest in Kilvarnet,
My brother in Mocharabuiee.

I passed my brother and cousin:
They read in their books of prayer;
I read in my book of songs
I bought at the Sligo fair.

When we come at the end of time
To Peter sitting in state,
He will smile on the three old spirits,
But call me first through the gate;

For the good are always the merry,
Save by an evil chance,
And the merry love the fiddle,
And the merry love to dance:

And when the folk there spy me,
They will all come up to me,
With 'Here is the fiddler of Dooney!'
And dance like a wave of the sea.

W. B. YEATS

Green Man in the Garden

Green man in the garden
 Staring from the tree,
Why do you look so long and hard
 Through the pane at me?

Your eyes are dark as holly,
 Of sycamore your horns,
Your bones are made of elder-branch,
 Your teeth are made of thorns.

Your hat is made of ivy-leaf,
 Of bark your dancing shoes,
And evergreen and green and green
 Your jacket and shirt and trews.

Leave your house and leave your land
 And throw away the key,
 And never look behind, he creaked,
 And come and live with me.

I bolted up the window,
 I bolted up the door,
I drew the blind that I should find
 The green man never more.

But when I softly turned the stair
 As I went up to bed,
I saw the green man standing there.
 Sleep well, my friend, he said.

CHARLES CAUSLEY

[34]

The Ballad of Barnaby

Listen, good people, and you shall hear
A story of old that will gladden your ear,
The Tale of Barnaby, who was, they say,
The finest tumbler of his day.

In every town great crowds he drew,
And all men marvelled to see him do
The French Vault, the Vault of Champagne,
The Vault of Metz, and the Vault of Lorraine.

His eyes were blue, his figure was trim,
He liked the girls and the girls liked him;
For years he lived a life of vice,
Drinking in taverns and throwing the dice.

It happened one day he was riding along
Between two cities, whistling a song,
When he saw what then was quite common to see,
Two ravens perched on a gallows-tree.

'Barnaby,' the first raven began,
'Will one day be as this hanging man':
'Yes,' said the other, 'and we know well
That when that day comes he will go to Hell.'

Then Barnaby's conscience smote him sore;
He repented of all he had done heretofore:
'Woe is me! I will forsake
This wicked world and penance make.'

The evening air was grave and still
When he came to a monastery built on a hill:
As its bells the Angelus did begin,
He knocked at the door and they let him in.

(Choral music)

The monks in that place were men of parts,
Learned in the sciences and the arts:
The Abbot could logically define
The place of all creatures in the Scheme Divine.

Brother Maurice then wrote down all that he said
In a flowing script that it might be read,
And Brother Alexander adorned the book
With pictures that gave it a beautiful look.

There were brothers there who could compose
Latin Sequences in verse and prose,
And a brother from Picardy, too, who sung
The praise of Our Lady in the vulgar tongue.

(Choral music)

Now Barnaby had never learned to read,
Nor *Paternoster* knew nor *Creed*;
Watching them all at work and prayer,
Barnaby's heart began to despair.

Down to the crypt at massing-time
He crept like a man intent on crime:
In a niche there above the altar stood
A statue of Our Lady carved in wood.

'Blessed Virgin,' he cried, 'enthroned on high,
Ignorant as a beast am I:
Tumbling is all I have learnt to do;
Mother-of-God, let me tumble for You.'

Straightway he stripped off his jerkin,
And his tumbling acts he did begin:
So eager was he to do Her honor
That he vaulted higher than ever before.

[36]

(Ballet music)

The French Vault, the Vault of Champagne,
The Vault of Metz and the Vault of Lorraine,
He did them all till he sank to the ground,
His body asweat and his head in a swound.

Unmarked by him, Our Lady now
Steps down from Her niche and wipes his brow.
'Thank you, Barnaby,' She said and smiled;
'Well have you tumbled for me, my child.'

From then on at the Office-Hours
Barnaby went to pay Her his devoirs.
One brother thought to himself: 'Now where
Does Barnaby go at our times of prayer?'

And so next day when Barnaby slipped
Away he followed him down to the crypt.
When he saw how he honored the Mother-of-God,
This brother thought: 'This is very odd.

It may be well: I believe it is,
But the Abbot, surely, should know of this.'
To the Abbot he went with reverent mien
And told him exactly what he had seen.

The Abbot said to him: 'Say no word
To the others of what you have seen and heard.
I will come to-morrow and watch with you
Before I decide what I ought to do.'

Next day behind a pillar they hid,
And the Abbot marked all that Barnaby did.
Watching him leap and vault and tumble,
He thought, 'This man is holy and humble.'

[37]

(Ballet music)

'Lady,' cried Barnaby, 'I beg of Thee
To intercede with Thy Son for me!',
Gave one more leap, then down he dropped,
And lay dead still, for his heart had stopped.

Then grinning demons, black as coal,
Swarmed out of Hell to seize his soul:
'In vain shall be his pious fuss,
For every tumbler belongs to us.'

(Ballet music)

But Our Lady and Her angels held them at bay,
With shining swords they drove them away,
And Barnaby's soul they bore aloft,
Singing with voices sweet and soft.

CHORUS: *Gloria in excelsis Deo.*

W. H. AUDEN

Joshua Fit de Battle of Jerico

Joshua fit de battle of Jerico,
Jerico, Jerico,
Joshua fit de battle of Jerico,
An' de walls come tumblin' down.

You may talk about yo' king of Gideon,
You may talk about yo' man of Saul,
Dere's none like good ol' Joshua
At de battle of Jerico.

Up to de walls of Jerico
He marched with spear in han'
'Go blow dem ram horns,' Joshua cried
'Cause de battle am in my han'.'

Den de lam'ram sheep horns begin to blow,
Trumpets begin to soun',
Joshua commanded de chillen to shout,
An' de walls come tumblin' down.

Dat mornin' Joshua fit de battle of Jerico,
Jerico, Jerico,
Joshua fit de battle of Jerico,
An' de walls come tumblin' down.

ANONYMOUS

Abou Ben Adhem

Abou Ben Adhem (may his tribe increase!)
Awoke one night from a deep dream of peace,
And saw, within the moonlight in his room,
Making it rich, and like a lily in bloom,
An angel writing in a book of gold: –
Exceeding peace had made Ben Adhem bold,
And to the presence in the room he said,
'What writest thou?' The vision raised its head,
And with a look made of all sweet accord,
Answered, 'The names of those who love the Lord.'
'And is mine one?' said Abou. 'Nay, not so,'
Replied the angel. Abou spoke more low,
But cheerly still; and said, 'I pray thee, then,
Write me as one that loves his fellow men.'

The angel wrote, and vanished. The next night
It came again with a great wakening light,
And showed the names whom love of God had blest,
And lo! Ben Adhem's name led all the rest.

LEIGH HUNT

'Mips and ma'
(from 'Praise to the End')

Mips and ma the mooly moo,
The likes of him is biting who,
A cow's a care and who's a coo? –
What footie does is final.

My dearest dear my fairest fair,
Your father tossed a cat in air,
Though neither you nor I was there, –
What footie does is final.

Be large as an owl, be slick as a frog,
Be good as a goose, be big as a dog,
Be sleek as a heifer, be long as a hog, –
What footie will do will be final.

THEODORE ROETHKE

Humpty Dumpty's Recitation

In winter, when the fields are white,
I sing this song for your delight –

In spring, when woods are getting green,
I'll try and tell you what I mean.

In summer, when the days are long,
Perhaps you'll understand the song:

In autumn, when the leaves are brown,
Take pen and ink, and write it down.

I sent a message to the fish:
I told them 'This is what I wish.'

The little fishes of the sea
They sent an answer back to me.

The little fishes' answer was
'We cannot do it, Sir, because —'

I sent to them again to say
'It will be better to obey.'

The fishes answered with a grin,
'Why, what a temper you are in!'

I told them once, I told them twice:
They would not listen to advice.

I took a kettle large and new,
Fit for the deed I had to do.

My heart went hop, my heart went thump;
I filled the kettle at the pump.

Then someone came to me and said
'The little fishes are in bed.'

I said to him, I said it plain,
'Then you must wake them up again.'

I said it very loud and clear;
I went and shouted in his ear.

But he was very stiff and proud;
He said 'You needn't shout so loud!'

And he was very proud and stiff;
He said 'I'd go and wake them, if –'

I took a corkscrew from the shelf:
I went to wake them up myself.

And when I found the door was locked,
I pulled and pushed and kicked and knocked.

And when I found the door was shut,
I tried to turn the handle, but –

LEWIS CARROLL

Sliver

Cheap little rhymes
A cheap little tune
Are sometimes as dangerous
As a sliver of the moon.
A cheap little tune
To cheap little rhymes
Can cut a man's
Throat sometimes.

LANGSTON HUGHES

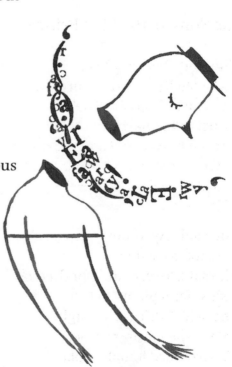

A Riddle

Bag of bones,
Old bony,
Who'd be you for love or money?
Yet for neither love
Nor money,
You'll be mine,
My Bony.

JOHN MOLE

The Song of the Mad Prince

Who said, 'Peacock Pie'?
    The old King to the sparrow:
Who said, 'Crops are ripe'?
    Rust to the harrow:
Who said, 'Where sleeps she now?
    Where rests she now her head,
Bathed in eve's loveliness'? –
    That's what I said.

Who said, 'Ay, mum's the word';
    Sexton to willow:
Who said, 'Green dusk for dreams,
    Moss for a pillow'?
Who said, 'All Time's delight
    Hath she for narrow bed;
Life's troubled bubble broken' –
    That's what I said.

WALTER DE LA MARE

Purkis

The red king lay in the black grove:
The red blood dribbled on moss and beech-mast.

With reversed horseshoes, Tyrrel has gone
Across the ford, scuds on the tossing channel.

Call the birds to their dinner. 'Not I,' said the hoarse crow,
'Not I,' whistled the red kite
'Will peck from their sockets those glazing eyes.'

Who will give him to his grave? 'Not I,' said the beetle
'Will shift one gram of ground under his corpse,
Nor plant in his putrid flank my progeny.'

Robin, red robin, will you in charity
Strew red Will with the fallen leaves?

'I cover the bodies of Christian men:
He lies unhouseled in the wilderness,
The desolation that his father made.'

Purkis came by in his charcoal-cart:
'He should lie in Winchester. I will tug him there –
Canons and courtiers perhaps will tip me,
A shilling or two for the charcoal-burner.'

Purkis trundled through the town gates,
And 'Coals!' he cried, 'coals, coals, coals,
Coals, charcoal, dry sticks for the burning!'

JOHN HEATH-STUBBS

O Why Am I so Bright

O why am I so bright
Flying in the night?

Why am I so fair
Flying through the air?

Will you let me in
After all I've done?

You are a good boy
On the fields of joy.

We see you as you go
Across the fields of snow.

We will not let you in.
Never. Never. Never.

W. S. GRAHAM

Lower the Diver

Lower the diver over the side
Down to the roots of the swirling tide.

Lower the diver, weighted with lead,
Glass and brass helmet over his head.

Lower the diver on to the deck
And the barnacled masts of the long-lost wreck.

Lower the diver; will he find jars,
Rust-sealed treasure-chests, silver bars?

Lower the diver; will he find gold,
Cannon-balls, skulls, or an empty hold?

Lower the diver; pray that the shark
Doesn't mind guests in the salty dark.

Lower the diver; then man the winch,
Wind him up slowly, inch by inch.

Undo his helmet. Why does he weep?
Is it so bad to be hauled from the deep?

Talk to the diver. What does he mean –
'Mermaids are real and her eyes were green'?

RICHARD EDWARDS

The Song of Wandering Aengus

I went out to the hazel wood,
Because a fire was in my head,
And cut and peeled a hazel wand,
And hooked a berry to a thread;

And when white moths were on the wing,
And moth-like stars were flickering out,
I dropped the berry in a stream
And caught a little silver trout.

When I had laid it on the floor
I went to blow the fire aflame,
But something rustled on the floor,
And some one called me by my name;
It had become a glimmering girl
With apple blossom in her hair
Who called me by my name and ran
And faded through the brightening air.

Though I am old with wandering
Through hollow lands and hilly lands,
I will find out where she has gone,
And kiss her lips and take her hands;
And walk among long dappled grass,
And pluck till time and times are done
The silver apples of the moon,
The golden apples of the sun.

W. B. YEATS

'Come into the orchard, Anne'

Come into the orchard, Anne,
    For the dark owl, Night, has fled,
And Phosphor slumbers, as well as he can
    With a daffodil sky for a bed:
And the musk of the roses perplexes a man,
    And the pimpernel muddles his head.

A. C. SWINBURNE

[47]

Calico Pie

I

Calico Pie,
The little Birds fly
Down to the calico tree,
   Their wings were blue,
   And they sang 'Tilly-loo!'
Till away they flew –
     And they never came back to me!
       They never came back!
       They never came back!
     They never came back to me!

II

Calico Jam,
The little Fish swam,
Over the syllabub sea,
        He took off his hat,
     To the Sole and the Sprat,
     And the Willeby-wat, –
But he never came back to me!
     He never came back!
     He never came back!
He never came back to me!

III

Calico Ban,
The little Mice ran,
To be ready in time for tea,
   Flippity flup,
   They drank it all up,

And danced in the cup, –
But they never came back to me!
  They never came back!
  They never came back!
They never came back to me!

IV

Calico Drum,
  The Grasshoppers come,
The Butterfly, Beetle, and Bee,
  Over the ground,
  Around and round,
  With a hop and a bound, –
But they never came back!
  They never came back!
  They never came back!
They never came back to me!

EDWARD LEAR

Nothing Poem

There's nothing in the Garden,
and unless I'm losing my sight,
there was nothing again this morning.
It must have been there all night

It's hard to see a nothing
or even where it's been.
This was the longest nothing
that I have ever seen.

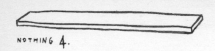

I locked all the drink in the cellar
so nothing could get at the gin,
but by skwonkle o'clock in the evening
nothing had got in!

So I bolted the doors and windows
so nothing could escape,
I called for the local policeman
who was armed with a helmet and cape

NOTHING 5.

nothing 6.

'I hear there's been a break in
and you might have lost something of worth.
Can you describe the intruder?'
'Yes, he looks like nothing on earth!'

SPIKE MILLIGAN

N○THING 7.

NOTHING 8.

'A Bird came down the Walk'

A Bird came down the Walk –
He did not know I saw –
He bit an Angleworm in halves
And ate the fellow, raw,

And then he drank a Dew
From a convenient Grass –
And then hopped sidewise to the Wall
To let a Beetle pass –

He glanced with rapid eyes
That hurried all around –
They looked like frightened Beads, I thought –
He stirred his Velvet Head

Like one in danger, Cautious,
I offered him a Crumb
And he unrolled his feathers
And rowed him softer home –

Than Oars divide the Ocean,
Too silver for a seam –
Or Butterflies, off Banks of Noon
Leap, plashless as they swim.

EMILY DICKINSON

Two Cuckoo Rhymes

Cuck-òo, Cuck-òo!
What do you do?
   'In April

I open my bill;
    In May
I sing night and day;
    In June
I change my tune;
    In July
Far – far I fly;
    In August
Away I *must*.'

The cuckoo he's a fine bird,
    He sings as he flies;
He brings us good tidings;
    He tells us no lies;

He sucks little birds' eggs
    To make his voice clear;
And when he sings *Cuck-oo*!
    The summer is near.

ANONYMOUS

The Song of the Dumb Waiter

Who went to sleep in the flower-bed?
Who let the fire-dog out of the shed?

Who sailed the sauce-boat down the stream?
What did the railway-sleeper dream?

Who was it chopped the boot-tree down,
And rode the clothes-horse through the town?

JAMES REEVES

The Old Sailor

There came an old sailor
Who sat to sup
Under the trees
Of the *Golden Cup*.

Beer in a mug
And a slice of cheese
With a hunk of bread
He munched at his ease.

Then in the summer
Dusk he lit
A little black pipe,
And sucked at it.

He thought of his victuals,
Of ships, the sea,
Of his home in the West,
And his children three.

And he stared and stared
To where, afar,
The lighthouse gleamed
At the harbour bar;

Till his pipe grew cold,
And down on the board
He laid his head,
And snored, snored, snored.

WALTER DE LA MARE

[53]

The Charcoal-Burner

The charcoal-burner has tales to tell.
He lives in the Forest,
Alone in the Forest;
He sits in the Forest,
Alone in the Forest.
And the sun comes slanting between the trees,
And rabbits come up, and they give him good-morning,
And rabbits come up and say, 'Beautiful morning' . . .
And the moon swings clear of the tall black trees,
And owls fly over and wish him good-night,
Quietly over to wish him good-night . . .

And he sits and thinks of the things they know,
He and the Forest, alone together –
The springs that come and the summers that go,
Autumn dew on bracken and heather,
The drip of the Forest beneath the snow . . .
All the things they have seen,
All the things they have heard:
An April sky swept clean and the song of a bird . . .
Oh, the charcoal-burner has tales to tell!
And he lives in the Forest and knows us well.

A. A. MILNE

The Frozen Man

Out at the edge of town
where black trees

crack their fingers
in the icy wind

and hedges freeze
on their shadows

and the breath of cattle,
still as boulders,

hangs in rags
under the rolling moon,

a man is walking
alone:

on the coal-black road
his cold

feet
ring

and
ring.

Here in a snug house
at the heart of town

the fire is burning
red and yellow and gold:

you can hear the warmth
like a sleeping cat

breathe softly
in every room.

When the frozen man
comes to the door,

let him in,
let him in,
let him in.

KIT WRIGHT

'There was an Old Man who said, "Well!" '

There was an Old Man who said, 'Well!
Will *nobody* answer this bell?
I have pulled day and night, till my hair has grown white,
But nobody answers this bell!'

EDWARD LEAR

Harold's Leap

Harold, are you asleep?
Harold, I remember your leap,
It may have killed you
But it was a brave thing to do.
Two promontories ran high into the sky,
He leapt from one rock to the other
And fell to the sea's smother.
Harold was always afraid to climb high,
But something urged him on,
He felt he should try.
I would not say that he was wrong,
Although he succeeded in doing nothing but die.
Would you?
Ever after that steep

Place was called Harold's Leap.
It was a brave thing to do.

STEVIE SMITH

'Amelia mixed the mustard'

Amelia mixed the mustard,
   She mixed it good and thick;
She put it in the custard
   And made her Mother sick,
And showing satisfaction
   By many a loud huzza
'Observe' said she 'the action
   Of mustard on Mamma.'

A. E. HOUSMAN

On the Death of a Female Officer of the Salvation Army

'Hallelujah!' was the only observation
That escaped Lieutenant-Colonel Mary Jane,
When she tumbled off the platform in the station,
And was cut in little pieces by the train.
   Mary Jane, the train is through yer,
   Hallelujah, Hallelujah!
We will gather up the fragments that remain.

A. E. HOUSMAN

[57]

On the Planet of Flies

On the Planet of Flies
it's a poor show for men.
What they do here to flies
flies there do to them.

Men find themselves sticking
on man-papers there,
or swim round and sink
in sugar and beer.

On some points I give
the prize to the flies,
we're not mistakenly swallowed
or cooked in their pies

CHRISTIAN MORGENSTERN
translated by Geoffrey Grigson

The Mad Gardener's Song

He thought he saw an Elephant,
    That practised on a fife:
He looked again, and found it was
    A letter from his wife.
'At length I realise,' he said,
    'The bitterness of Life!'

He thought he saw a Buffalo
    Upon the chimney-piece:
He looked again, and found it was
    His Sister's Husband's Niece.

[58]

'Unless you leave this house,' he said,
   'I'll send for the Police!'

He thought he saw a Rattlesnake
   That questioned him in Greek:
He looked again, and found it was
   The Middle of Next Week.
'The one thing I regret,' he said,
'Is that it cannot speak!'

He thought he saw a Banker's Clerk
   Descending from the bus:
He looked again, and found it was
   A Hippopotamus:
'If this should stay to dine,' he said,
   'There won't be much for us!'

He thought he saw a Kangaroo
    That worked a coffee-mill:
He looked again, and found it was
    A Vegetable-Pill.
'Were I to swallow this,' he said,
    'I should be very ill!'

He thought he saw a Coach-and-Four
    That stood beside his bed:
He looked again, and found it was
    A Bear without a Head.
'Poor thing,' he said, 'poor silly thing!
    It's waiting to be fed!'

He thought he saw an Albatross
    That fluttered round the lamp:
He looked again, and found it was
    A Penny-Postage-Stamp.
'You'd best be getting home,' he said:
    'The nights are very damp!'

He thought he saw a Garden-Door
    That opened with a key:
He looked again, and found it was
    A Double Rule of Three:
'And all its mystery,' he said,
    'Is clear as day to me!'

He thought he saw an Argument
    That proved he was the Pope:
He looked again, and found it was
    A Bar of Mottled Soap.
'A fact so dread,' he faintly said,
    'Extinguishes all hope!'

LEWIS CARROLL

April Fool

Here come I, old April Fool,
Between March hare and nuts in May.
Fool me forward, fool me back,
Hares will dance and nuts will crack.

Here come I, my fingers crossed
Between the shuffle and the deal.
Fool me flush or fool me straight,
Queens are wild and queens will wait.

Here come I, my clogs worn out
Between the burden and the song.
Fool me hither, fool me hence,
Keep the sound but ditch the sense.

Here come I, my hair on fire,
Between the devil and the deep.
Fool me over, fool me down,
Sea shall dry and devil shall drown.

Here come I, in guts and brass,
Between the raven and the pit.
Fool me under, fool me flat,
Coffins land on Ararat.

Here come I, old April Fool,
Between the hoar frost and the fall.
Fool me drunk or fool me dry,
Spring comes back, and back come I.

LOUIS MACNEICE

The Monotony Song

A donkey's tail is very nice
You mustn't pull it more than twice,
Now that's a piece of good advice
   – Heigho, meet Hugh and Harry!

One day Hugh walked up to a bear
And said, Old Boy, you're shedding hair,
And shedding more than here and there,
   – Heigho, we're Hugh and Harry!

The bear said, Sir, you go too far,
I wonder who you think you are
To make remarks about my – Grrrr!
   – And there was only Harry!

This Harry ran straight up a wall,
But found he wasn't there at all,
And so he had a horrid fall.
   – Alas, alack for Harry!

My sweetheart is a ugly witch,
And you should see her noses twitch, –
But Goodness Me, her father's rich!
   – And I'm not Hugh nor Harry!

This is, you see, a silly song
And you can sing it all day long –
You'll find I'm either right or wrong
   – Heigho Hugh and Harry!

The moral is, I guess you keep
Yourself awake until you sleep,
And sometimes look before you leap
   – Unless you're Hugh or Harry!

THEODORE ROETHKE

[62]

Off the Ground

Three jolly Farmers
Once bet a pound
Each dance the others would
Off the ground.
Out of their coats
They slipped right soon,
And neat and nicesome,
Put each his shoon.

One – two – three! –
And away they go,
Not too fast,
And not too slow;
Out from the elm-tree's
Noonday shadow,
Into the sun
And across the meadow.
Past the schoolroom,
With knees well bent
Fingers a-flicking,
They dancing went.
Up sides and over,
And round and round,
They crossed click-clacking,
The Parish bound.
By Tupman's meadow
They did their mile,
Tee-to-tum
On a three-barred stile.
Then straight through Whipham,
Downhill to Week,
Footing it lightsome,

But not too quick,
Up fields to Watchet,
And on through Wye,
Till seven fine churches
They'd seen skip by –
Seven fine churches,
And five old mills,
Farms in the valley,
And sheep on the hills;
Old Man's Acre
And Dead Man's Pool
All left behind,
As they danced through Wool.

And Wool gone by,
Like tops that seem
To spin in sleep
They danced in dream:
Withy – Wellover –
Wassop – Wo –
Like an old clock
Their heels did go.
A league and a league
And a league they went,
And not one weary,
And not one spent.
And lo, and behold!
Past Willow-cum-Leigh
Stretched with its waters
The great green sea.

Says Farmer Bates,
'I puffs and I blows,
What's under the water,

Why, no man knows!'
Says Farmer Giles,
'My wind comes weak,
And a good man drownded
Is far to seek.'
But Farmer Turvey,
On twirling toes
Ups with his gaiters,
And in he goes:
Down where the mermaids
Pluck and play
On their twangling harps
In a sea-green day;
Down where the mermaids,
Finned and fair,
Sleek with their combs
Their yellow hair . . .

Bates and Giles –
On the shingle sat,
Gazing at Turvey's
Floating hat.
But never a ripple
Nor bubble told
Where he was supping
Off plates of gold.
Never an echo
Rilled through the sea
Of the feasting and dancing
And minstrelsy.

They called – called – called:
Came no reply:
Nought but the ripples'

Sandy sigh.
Then glum and silent
They sat instead,
Vacantly brooding
On home and bed,
Till both together
Stood up and said: –
'Us knows not, dreams not,
Where you be,
Turvey, unless
In the deep blue sea;
But axcusing silver –
And it comes most willing –
Here's us two paying
Our forty shilling;
For it's sartin sure, Turvey,
Safe and sound,
You danced us square, Turvey;
Off the ground!'

WALTER DE LA MARE

Old Ballad

Oh, do not marry that wild young man,
    oh, do not marry, my daughter,
or you will live the rest of your days
    on dog biscuits and rain-water.

But marry that wild young man she did,
    glad that he could support her
on the best dog biscuits money could buy
    and the freshest of fresh rain-water.

CHRISTOPHER REID

[66]

'O what is that sound which so thrills the ear'

O what is that sound which so thrills the ear
  Down in the valley drumming, drumming?
Only the scarlet soldiers, dear,
    The soldiers coming.

O what is that light I see flashing so clear
  Over the distance brightly, brightly?
Only the sun on their weapons, dear,
    As they step lightly.

O what are they doing with all that gear;
  What are they doing this morning, this morning?
Only the usual manoeuvres, dear,
    Or perhaps a warning.

O why have they left the road down there;
  Why are they suddenly wheeling, wheeling?
Perhaps a change in the orders, dear;
    Why are you kneeling?

O haven't they stopped for the doctor's care;
  Haven't they reined their horses, their horses?
Why, they are none of them wounded, dear,
    None of these forces.

O is it the parson they want with white hair;
  Is it the parson, is it, is it?
No, they are passing his gateway, dear,
    Without a visit.

O it must be the farmer who lives so near;
  It must be the farmer so cunning, so cunning?
They have passed the farm already, dear,
    And now they are running.

[67]

O where are you going? stay with me here!
  Were the vows you swore me deceiving, deceiving?
No, I promised to love you, dear,
    But I must be leaving.

O it's broken the lock and splintered the door,
  O it's the gate where they're turning, turning;
Their feet are heavy on the floor
    And their eyes are burning.

W. H. AUDEN

Charm

The owl is abroad, the bat, and the toad,
  And so is the cat-a-mountayne,
The ant, and the mole sit both in a hole,
  And frog peeps out o'the fountayne;
The dogs, they do bay, and the timbrels play,
  The spindle is now a turning;
The moon it is red, and the stars are fled,
  But all the sky is a burning:

BEN JONSON

Death in Leamington

She died in the upstairs bedroom
  By the light of the ev'ning star
That shone through the plate glass window
  From over Leamington Spa.

Beside her the lonely crochet
    Lay patiently and unstirred,
But the fingers that would have work'd it
    Were dead as the spoken word.

And Nurse came in with the tea-things
    Breast high 'mid the stands and chairs –
But Nurse was alone with her own little soul,
    And the things were alone with theirs.

She bolted the big round window,
    She let the blinds unroll,
She set a match to the mantle,
    She covered the fire with coal.

And 'Tea!' she said in a tiny voice
    'Wake up! It's nearly *five*.'
Oh! Chintzy, chintzy cheeriness,
    Half dead and half alive!

Do you know that the stucco is peeling?
    Do you know that the heart will stop?
From those yellow Italianate arches
    Do you hear the plaster drop?

Nurse looked at the silent bedstead,
    At the grey, decaying face,
As the calm of a Leamington ev'ning
    Drifted into the place.

She moved the table of bottles
    Away from the bed to the wall;
And tiptoeing gently over the stairs
    Turned down the gas in the hall.

JOHN BETJEMAN

[69]

'why did you go'

why did you go
little fourpaws?
you forgot to shut
your big eyes.

where did you go?
like little kittens
are all the leaves
which open in the rain.

little kittens who
are called spring,
is what we stroke
maybe asleep?

do you know? or maybe did
something go away
ever so quietly
when we weren't looking.

    E. E. CUMMINGS

'hist whist'

hist   whist
little ghostthings
tip-toe
twinkle-toe

little twitchy
witches and tingling

[70]

goblins
hob-a-nob   hob-a-nob

little hoppy happy
toad in tweeds
tweeds
little itchy mousies

with scuttling
eyes   rustle and run   and
hidehidehide
whisk

whisk   look out for the old woman
with the wart on her nose
what she'll do to yer
nobody knows

for she knows the devil   ooch
the devil   ouch
the devil
ach   the great

green
dancing
devil
devil

devil
devil

      wheeEEE

E. E. CUMMINGS

[71]

The Devil's Swing

Beneath a shaggy fir tree,
Above a noisy stream
The devil's swing is swinging,
Pushed by his hairy hand.

He swings the swing while laughing,
　　Swing high, swing low,
　　Swing high, swing low,
The board is bent and creaking,
The rope is taut and chafing
Against a heavy branch.

The swaying board is rushing
With long and drawn-out creaks;
With hand on hip, the devil
Is laughing with a wheeze.

I clutch, I swoon, I'm swinging,
　　Swing high, swing low,
　　Swing high, swing low,
I'm clinging and I'm dangling,
And from the devil trying
To turn my languid gaze.

Above the dusky fir tree
The azure sky guffaws:
'You're caught upon the swings, love,
The devil take you, swing!'

Beneath the shaggy fir tree
The screeching throng whirls round:
'You're caught upon the swings, love,
The devil take you, swing!'

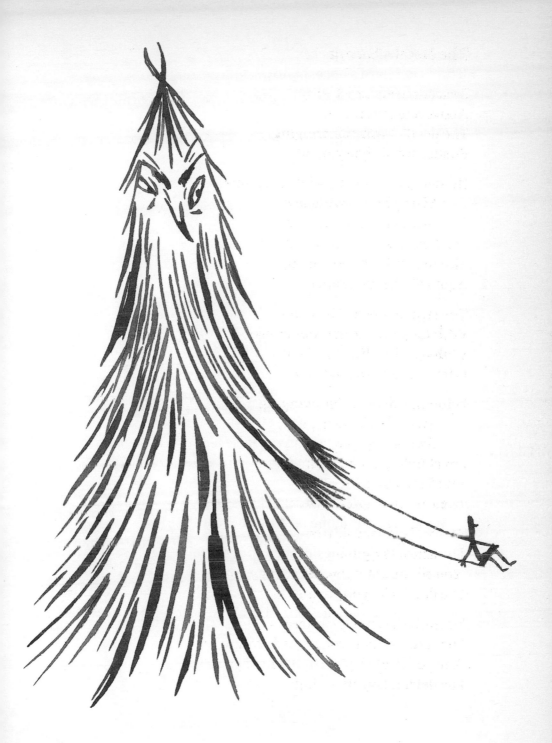

The devil will not slacken
The swift board's pace, I know,
Until his hand unseats me
With a ferocious blow.

Until the jute, while twisting,
Is frayed through till it breaks,
Until my ground beneath me
Turns upward to my face.

I'll fly above the fir tree
And fall flat on the ground.
So swing the swing, you devil,
Go higher, higher . . . oh!

FYODOR SOLOGUB
(translated by April FitzLyon)

The Old False Leg

Three crows hopped on an old false leg,
   On an old false leg,
   An old false leg,
Three crows hopped on an old false leg
   Which lay out alone on the moor.

Whoever could have dropped that old false leg,
   Old false leg,
   That old false leg,
Whoever could have dropped that old false leg,
   Out by the lake on the moor?

It was nobody dropped that old false leg,
   Old false leg,
   Old false leg,

It was nobody dropped that very false leg,
    Which slept out alone on the moor.

That old false leg jumped up on its toes,
    Up on its toes,
    Up on its toes,
That old false leg jumped up on its toes,
    In the very wet mist on the moor,

And it hit the tail feathers off those crows,
    Off those crows,
    Off those crows,
And it hit the tail feathers off those crows,
    Caw, caw, caw on the moor.

And those crows flew away quite nakedly,
    Quite nakedly,
    Quite nakedly,
And those crows flew away quite nakedly,
    Into the mist on the moor.

And the false leg thereupon strolled to the shore,
    Strolled to the shore,
    Strolled to the shore,
And the false leg thereupon strolled to the shore,
    Into the lake, and was seen no more,
    Seen no more.

GEOFFREY GRIGSON

The Angry Pigeon

A tramp shot a pigeon and cooked it to eat.
He carved off its left leg and one of its feet

Which he ate as he thought and he thought as he sat
That his hair and his thoughts were under his hat.

A tramp shot a pigeon and cooked it to eat.
He carved off its right leg and one of its feet
Which he ate as he thought and thought as he sat
That his thoughts were as thick as his hair in his hat.

A tramp shot a pigeon and ate its left wing
And as he was eating he started to sing
And he thought as he sang and he sang as he thought
That to sing with his mouthful was more than he ought.

A tramp shot a pigeon and ate its right wing
And as he was eating he started to sing
And he sang as he thought and he thought as he sang
How his meal had begun with a click and a bang.

A tramp shot a pigeon and cut off his head
Which opened its beak and angrily said,
'Do you know what you're doing, you bottle-nosed bumpkin?
You'll eat me completely. Sing marrow. Sing pumpkin.'

ERIC ROLLS

The King's Breakfast

The King asked
The Queen, and
The Queen asked
The Dairymaid:
'Could we have some butter for
The Royal slice of bread?'
The Queen asked

The Dairymaid,
The Dairymaid
Said, 'Certainly,
I'll go and tell
The cow
Now
Before she goes to bed.'

The Dairymaid
She curtsied,
And went and told
The Alderney:
'Don't forget the butter for
The Royal slice of bread.'
The Alderney
Said sleepily:
'You'd better tell
His Majesty
That many people nowadays
Like marmalade
Instead.'

The Dairymaid
Said, 'Fancy!'
And went to
Her Majesty.
She curtsied to the Queen, and
She turned a little red:
'Excuse me,
Your Majesty,
For taking of
The liberty,
But marmalade is tasty, if
It's very

Thickly
Spread.'

The Queen said
'Oh!'
And went to
His Majesty:
'Talking of the butter for
The Royal slice of bread,
Many people
Think that
Marmalade
Is nicer.
Would you like to try a little
Marmalade
Instead?'

The King said,
'Bother!'
And then he said,
'Oh, deary me!'
The King sobbed, 'Oh, deary me!'
And went back to bed.
'Nobody,'
He whimpered,
'Could call me
A fussy man;
I *only* want
A little bit
Of butter for
My bread!'

The Queen said,
'There, there!'

And went to
The Dairymaid.
The Dairymaid
Said, 'There, there!'
And went to the shed.
The cow said,
'There, there!
I didn't really
Mean it;
Here's milk for his porringer
And butter for his bread.'

The Queen took
The butter
And brought it to
His Majesty;
The King said,
'Butter, eh?'
And bounced out of bed.
'Nobody,' he said,
As he kissed her
Tenderly,
'Nobody,' he said,
As he slid down
The banisters,
'Nobody,
My darling,
Could call me
A fussy man –
BUT
I do like a little bit of butter to my bread!'

A. A. MILNE

'There was an old man in a tree'

There was an old man in a tree,
Whose whiskers were lovely to see;
But the birds of the air, pluck'd them perfectly bare,
To make themselves nests in that tree.

EDWARD LEAR

Roman Wall Blues

Over the heather the wet wind blows,
I've lice in my tunic and a cold in my nose.

The rain comes pattering out of the sky.
I'm a Wall soldier, I don't know why.

The mist creeps over the hard grey stone.
My girl's in Tungria; I sleep alone.

Aulus goes hanging around her place,
I don't like his manners, I don't like his face.

Piso's a Christian, he worships a fish;
There'd be no kissing if he had his wish.

She gave me a ring but I diced it away;
I want my girl and I want my pay.

When I'm a veteran with only one eye
I shall do nothing but look at the sky.

W. H. AUDEN

The Listeners

'Is there anybody there?' said the Traveller,
    Knocking on the moonlit door;
And his horse in the silence champed the grasses
    Of the forest's ferny floor:
And a bird flew up out of the turret,
    Above the Traveller's head:
And he smote upon the door again a second time;
    'Is there anybody there?' he said.

But no one descended to the Traveller;
    No head from the leaf-fringed sill
Leaned over and looked into his grey eyes,
    Where he stood perplexed and still.
But only a host of phantom listeners
    That dwelt in the lone house then
Stood listening in the quiet of the moonlight
    To that voice from the world of men:
Stood thronging the faint moonbeams on the dark stair,
    That goes down to the empty hall,
Hearkening in an air stirred and shaken
    By the lonely Traveller's call.
And he felt in his heart their strangeness,
    Their stillness answering his cry,
While his horse moved, cropping the dark turf,
    'Neath the starred and leafy sky;
For he suddenly smote on the door, even
    Louder, and lifted his head: –
'Tell them I came, and no one answered,
    That I kept my word,' he said.
Never the least stir made the listeners,
    Though every word he spake
Fell echoing through the shadowiness of the still house
    From the one man left awake:
Ay, they heard his foot upon the stirrup,
    And the sound of iron on stone,
And how the silence surged softly backward,
    When the plunging hoofs were gone.

WALTER DE LA MARE

Hi!

Hi! handsome hunting man
Fire your little gun.
Bang! Now the animal
Is dead and dumb and done.
Nevermore to peep again, creep again, leap again,
Eat or sleep or drink again, Oh, what fun!

WALTER DE LA MARE

The Lady and the Bear

A Lady came to a Bear by a Stream.
'O why are you fishing that way?
Tell me, dear Bear there by the Stream,
Why are you fishing that way?'

'I am what is known as a Biddly Bear, –
That's why I'm fishing this way.
We Biddly's are Pee-culiar Bears.
And so, – I'm fishing this way.

'And besides, it seems there's a Law:
A most, most exactious Law
Says a Bear
Doesn't dare
Doesn't dare
Doesn't DARE
Use a Hook or a Line,
Or an old piece of Twine,
Not even the end of his Claw, Claw, Claw,
Not even the end of his Claw.
Yes, a Bear has to fish with his Paw, Paw, Paw.
A Bear has to fish with his Paw.'

[83]

'O it's Wonderful how with a flick of your Wrist,
You can fish out a fish, out a fish, out a fish,
If *I* were a fish I just couldn't resist
You, when you are fishing that way, that way,
When you are fishing that way.'

And at that the Lady slipped from the Bank
And fell in the Stream still clutching a Plank,
But the Bear just sat there until she Sank;
As he went on fishing his way, his way,
As he went on fishing his way.

THEODORE ROETHKE

The Table and the Chair

I

Said the Table to the Chair,
'You can hardly be aware,
'How I suffer from the heat,
'And from chilblains on my feet!
'If we took a little walk,
'We might have a little talk!
'Pray let us take the air!'
Said the Table to the Chair.

II

Said the Chair unto the Table,
'Now you *know* we are not able!
'How foolishly you talk,
'When you know *we cannot* walk!'
Said the Table, with a sigh,
'It can do no harm to try,
'I've as many legs as you,
'Why can't we walk on two?'

III

So they both went slowly down,
And walked about the town
With a cheerful bumpy sound,
As they toddled round and round.
And everybody cried,
As they hastened to their side,
'See! the Table and the Chair
'Have come out to take the air!'

IV

But in going down an alley,
To a castle in a valley,
They completely lost their way,
And wandered all the day,
Till, to see them safely back,
They paid a Ducky-quack,
And a Beetle, and a Mouse,
Who took them to their house.

V

Then they whispered to each other,
'O delightful little brother!
'What a lovely walk we've taken!
'Let us dine on Beans and Bacon!'
So the Ducky, and the leetle
Browny-Mousy and the Beetle
Dined, and danced upon their heads
Till they toddled to their beds.

EDWARD LEAR

A Crime to Report

I've a crime to report –
The rowan-tree said –
The theft of some berries,
Small, round, red.
It happened this morning –
Kids, I suppose –
I was tired from the gale
And having a doze.

A difficult case –
The policeman said,
Licking his pencil
And scratching his head –
We'll send down forensics
To search for clues:
Fingerprints, tyre marks,
The imprint of shoes,
But, if you ask me,

[86]

This berrying job
Sounds like the work
Of the Mistle Thrush mob.
We'll do what we can –
But a word to the wise –
Get some insurance,
And watch the skies.

RICHARD EDWARDS

The Knee on Its Own

A Lone Knee wanders through the world,
   A knee and nothing more;
It's not a tent, it's not a tree,
   A knee and nothing more.

In battle once there was a man
   Shot foully through and through;
The knee alone remained unhurt
   As saints are said to do.

Since then it's wandered through the world,
   A knee and nothing more.
It's not a tent, it's not a tree,
   A knee and nothing more.

CHRISTIAN MORGENSTERN
(translated by R. F. C. Hull)

'Alice is gone'

Alice is gone and I'm alone,
   Nobody understands
How lovely were her Fire Alarms,
   How fair her German Bands.

O how I cried when Alice died
   The day we were to have wed.
We never had our Roasted Duck
   And now she's a Loaf of Bread.

At nights I weep, I cannot sleep:
   Moonlight to me recalls
I never saw her Waterfront
   Nor she my Waterfalls.

W. H. AUDEN

Poker

A skeleton
on the sea-bed,
a bullet-hole
in its bone head.

Three queens
in its claw hand,
a black ace
on the pale sand.

A fish swims
near a fourth queen

[88]

where a shirt sleeve
would have once been.

CAROL ANN DUFFY

Sun a-shine, rain a-fall

Sun a-shine an' rain a-fall,
The Devil an' him wife cyan 'gree at all,
The two o' them want one fish-head,
The Devil call him wife bonehead,
She hiss her teeth, call him cock-eye,
Greedy, worthless an' workshy,
While them busy callin' name,
The puss walk in, sey is a shame
To see a nice fish go to was'e,
Lef' with a big grin pon him face.

VALERIE BLOOM

Song of the Death-Watch Beetle

Here come I, the death-watch beetle
Chewing away at the great cathedral;

Gnawing the mediaeval beams
And the magnificent carved rood screen

Gorging on gospels and epistles
From the illuminated missals;

As once I ate the odes of Sappho
And the histories of Manetho,

The lost plays of Euripides
And all the thought of Parmenides.

The Sibyl's leaves which the wind scattered,
And great aunt Delia's love letters.

Turn down the lamp in the cooling room:
There stand I with my little drum.

Death. Watch. You are watching death.
Blow out the lamp with your last breath.

JOHN HEATH-STUBBS

The Cat and the Moon

The cat went here and there
And the moon spun round like a top,
And the nearest kin of the moon,
The creeping cat, looked up.
Black Minnaloushe stared at the moon,
For, wander and wail as he would,

The pure cold light in the sky
Troubled his animal blood.
Minnaloushe runs in the grass
Lifting his delicate feet.
Do you dance, Minnaloushe, do you dance?
When two close kindred meet,
What better than call a dance?
Maybe the moon may learn,
Tired of that courtly fashion,
A new dance turn.
Minnaloushe creeps through the grass
From moonlit place to place,
The sacred moon overhead
Has taken a new phase.
Does Minnaloushe know that his pupils
Will pass from change to change,
And that from round to crescent,
From crescent to round they range?
Minnaloushe creeps through the grass
Alone, important and wise,
And lifts to the changing moon
His changing eyes.

W. B. YEATS

'I started Early'

I started Early – Took my Dog –
And visited the Sea –
The Mermaids in the Basement
Came out to look at me –

And Frigates – in the Upper Floor
Extended Hempen Hands –
Presuming Me to be a Mouse –
Aground – upon the Sands –

But no Man moved Me – till the Tide
Went past my simple Shoe –
And past my Apron – and my Belt
And past my Bodice – too –

And made as He would eat me up –
As wholly as a Dew
Upon a Dandelion's Sleeve –
And then – I started – too –

And He – He followed – close behind –
I felt His Silver Heel
Upon my Ankle – Then my Shoes
Would overflow with Pearl –

Until We met the Solid Town –
No One He seemed to know –
And bowing – with a Mighty look –
At me – The Sea withdrew –

EMILY DICKINSON

Overheard on a Saltmarsh

Nymph, nymph, what are your beads?

Green glass, goblin. Why do you stare at them?

Give them me.

       No.

Give them me. Give them me.

          No.

Then I will howl all night in the reeds,
Lie in the mud and howl for them.

Goblin, why do you love them so?

They are better than stars or water,
Better than voices of winds that sing,
Better than any man's fair daughter,
Your green glass beads on a silver ring.

Hush, I stole them out of the moon.

Give me your beads, I want them.

            No.

I will howl in a deep lagoon
For your green glass beads, I love them so.
Give them me. Give them.

        No.

HAROLD MONRO

[93]

They Call to One Another

They call to one another
    in the prisons of the sea
the mermen and mermaidens
    bound under lock and key
down in the green and salty dens
    and dungeons of the sea,
lying about in chains but
    dying to be free:
and this is why shortsighted men
    believe them not to be
for down to their dark dungeons it
    is very hard to see.
But sometimes morning fishermen
    drag up in the net
bits of bright glass or the silver comb
    of an old vanity set
or a letter rather hard to read
    because it is still wet
sent to remind us never, never
    never to forget
the mermen and mermaidens
    in the prisons of the sea
who call to one another
    when the stars of morning rise
and the stars of evening set
    for I have heard them calling
and I can hear them, yet.

GEORGE BARKER

[94]

Song Sung by a Man on a Barge to Another Man on a Different Barge in order to Drive him Mad

Oh,

I am the best bargee bar none,
You are the best bargee bar one!
You are the second-best bargee,
You are the best bargee bar me!

Oh,

I am the best . . .

(and so on, until he is
hurled into the canal)

    KIT WRIGHT

Lines Written by a Bear of Very Little Brain

On Monday, when the sun is hot
I wonder to myself a lot:
'Now is it true, or is it not,
That what is which and which is what?

On Tuesday, when it hails and snows,
The feeling on me grows and grows
That hardly anybody knows
If those are these or these are those.

On Wednesday, when the sky is blue,
And I have nothing else to do,
I sometimes wonder if it's true
That who is what and what is who.

On Thursday, when it starts to freeze
And hoar-frost twinkles on the trees,
How very readily one sees
That these are whose – but whose are these?

On Friday –
On Friday –
On Friday –
'What did happen on Friday?'

A. A. MILNE

The Song of the Jellicles

Jellicle Cats come out tonight,
Jellicle Cats come one come all:
The Jellicle Moon is shining bright –
Jellicles come to the Jellicle Ball.

Jellicle Cats are black and white,
Jellicle Cats are rather small;
Jellicle Cats are merry and bright,
And pleasant to hear when they caterwaul.
Jellicle Cats have cheerful faces,
Jellicle Cats have bright black eyes;
They like to practise their airs and graces
And wait for the Jellicle Moon to rise.

Jellicle Cats develop slowly,
Jellicle Cats are not too big;
Jellicle Cats are roly-poly,
They know how to dance a gavotte and a jig.
Until the Jellicle Moon appears

They make their toilette and take their repose:
Jellicles wash behind their ears,
Jellicles dry between their toes.

Jellicle Cats are white and black,
Jellicle Cats are of moderate size;
Jellicles jump like a jumping-jack,
Jellicle Cats have moonlit eyes.
They're quiet enough in the morning hours,
They're quiet enough in the afternoon,
Reserving their terpsichorean powers
To dance by the light of the Jellicle Moon.

Jellicle Cats are black and white,
Jellicle Cats (as I said) are small;
If it happens to be a stormy night
They will practise a caper or two in the hall.
If it happens the sun is shining bright
You would say they had nothing to do at all:
They are resting and saving themselves to be right
For the Jellicle Moon and the Jellicle Ball.

T. S. ELIOT

The Mules

In the world of mules
There are no rules.

OGDEN NASH

The Wapiti

There goes the Wapiti,
Hippety-hoppity!

OGDEN NASH

Song of the Hat-raising Doll

I raise my hat
And lower it.
As I unwind
I slow a bit.
This life –
I make a go of it
But tick-tock time
I know of it.

Yes, tick-tock time
I know of it.
I fear the final
O of it,
But making
A brave show of it
I raise my hat
And lower it.

JOHN MOLE

O, Dear

O, dear, O!
My cake's all dough,
And how to make it better
I do not know.

ANONYMOUS

Time to Rise

A birdie with a yellow bill
Hopped upon the window sill,
Cocked his shining eye and said:
'Ain't you 'shamed, you sleepy-head?'

ROBERT LOUIS STEVENSON

The Brave Man

The sun, that brave man,
Comes through boughs that lie in wait,
That brave man.

Green and gloomy eyes
In dark forms of the grass
Run away.

The good stars,
Pale helms and spiky spurs,
Run away.

Fears of my bed,
Fears of life and fears of death,
Run away.

That brave man comes up
From below and walks without meditation,
That brave man.

WALLACE STEVENS

Clock a Clay

In the cowslips peeps I lye
Hidden from the buzzing fly
While green grass beneath me lies
Pearled wi' dew like fishes eyes
Here I lye a Clock a clay
Waiting for the time o' day

While grassy forests quake surprise
And the wild wind sobs and sighs
My gold home rocks as like to fall
On its pillars green and tall
When the pattering rain drives bye
Clock a Clay keeps warm and dry

Day by day and night by night
All the week I hide from sight
In the cowslips peeps I lye
In rain and dew still warm and dry
Day and night and night and day
Red black spotted clock a clay

My home it shakes in wind and showers
Pale green pillar top't wi' flowers
Bending at the wild winds breath
Till I touch the grass beneath
Here still I live lone clock a clay
Watching for the time of day

JOHN CLARE

Toad

Stop looking like a purse. How could a purse
squeeze under the rickety door and sit,
full of satisfaction, in a man's house?

You clamber towards me on your four corners –
right hand, left foot, left hand, right foot.

I love you for being a toad,
for crawling like a Japanese wrestler,
and for not being frightened.

I put you in my purse hand, not shutting it,
and set you down outside directly under
every star.

A jewel in your head? Toad,
you've put one in mine,
a tiny radiance in a dark place.

NORMAN MACCAIG

Mooses

The goofy Moose, the walking house-frame,
Is lost
In the forest. He bumps, he blunders, he stands.

With massy bony thoughts sticking out near his ears –
Reaching out palm upwards, to catch whatever might be falling
    from heaven –
He tries to think,
Leaning their huge weight
On the lectern of his front legs.

He can't find the world!
Where did it go? What does a world look like?
The Moose
Crashes on, and crashes into a lake, and stares at the mountain
    and cries:
'Where do I belong? This is no place!'

He turns dragging half the lake out after him
And charges the cackling underbrush –

He meets another Moose
He stares, he thinks: 'It's only a mirror!'

'Where is the world?' he groans. 'O my lost world!
And why am I so ugly?
And why am I so far away from my feet?'

He weeps.
Hopeless drops drip from his droopy lips.

The other Moose just stands there doing the same.

Two dopes of the deep woods.

TED HUGHES

The Gondoliers of Greenland

The Gondoliers of Greenland
Are the Grumpiest folk in the North
Their canals melt on August the Second
And freeze up on August the Fourth.
In those two laborious glorious days
All their incomes must be made
And the rest of the year they wait listlessly
To ply their ridiculous trade.

ADRIAN MITCHELL

Snow in the Suburbs

Every branch big with it,
Bent every twig with it;
Every fork like a white web-foot;
Every street and pavement mute:
Some flakes have lost their way, and grope back upward, when
Meeting those meandering down they turn and descend again.
The palings are glued together like a wall,
And there is no waft of wind with the fleecy fall.

A sparrow enters the tree,
Whereon immediately
A snow-lump thrice his own slight size
Descends on him and showers his head and eyes,
And overturns him,
And near inurns him,
And lights on a nether twig, when its brush
Starts off a volley of other lodging lumps with a rush.

The steps are a blanched slope,
Up which, with feeble hope,
A black cat comes, wide-eyed and thin;
    And we take him in.

THOMAS HARDY

'There was a man of double deed'

There was a man of double deed
Who sowed his garden full of seed.
When the seed began to grow,
'Twas like a garden full of snow.
When the snow began to melt
'Twas like a ship without a bell.
When the ship began to sail,
'Twas like a bird without a tail.
When the bird began to fly,
'Twas like an eagle in the sky.
When the sky began to roar,
'Twas like a lion at the door.
When the door began to crack,
'Twas like a stick across my back.
When my back began to smart,
'Twas like a penknife in my heart.
When my heart began to bleed,
'Twas death, and death, and death indeed.

ANONYMOUS

Ballad of the Bread Man

Mary stood in the kitchen
　　Baking a loaf of bread.
An angel flew in through the window.
　　'We've a job for you,' he said.

'God in his big gold heaven,
　　Sitting in his big blue chair,
Wanted a mother for his little son.
　　Suddenly saw you there.'

Mary shook and trembled,
　　'It isn't true what you say.'
'Don't say that,' said the angel.
　　'The baby's on its way.'

Joseph was in the workshop
  Planing a piece of wood.
'The old man's past it,' the neighbours said.
  'That girl's been up to no good.'

'And who was that elegant fellow,'
  They said, 'in the shiny gear?'
The things they said about Gabriel
  Were hardly fit to hear.

Mary never answered,
  Mary never replied.
She kept the information,
  Like the baby, safe inside.

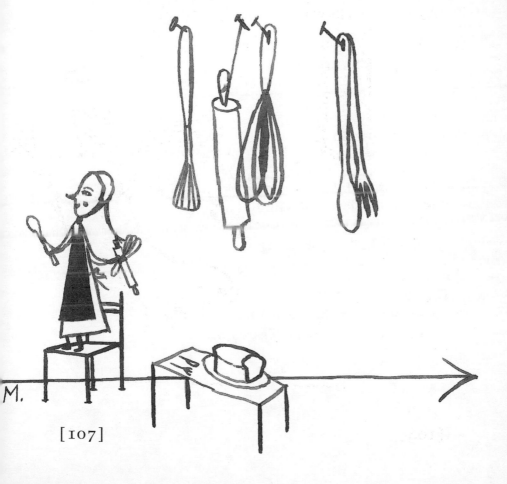

M.

It was election winter.
    They went to vote in town.
When Mary found her time had come
    The hotels let her down.

The baby was born in an annexe
    Next to the local pub.
At midnight, a delegation
    Turned up from the Farmers' Club.

They talked about an explosion
    That made a hole in the sky,
Said they'd been sent to the Lamb & Flag
    To see God come down from on high.

A few days later a bishop
    And a five-star general were seen
With the head of an African country
    In a bullet-proof limousine.

'We've come,' they said, 'with tokens
    For the little boy to choose.'
Told the tale about war and peace
    In the television news.

After them came the soldiers
    With rifle and bomb and gun,
Looking for enemies of the state.
    The family had packed and gone.

When they got back to the village
    The neighbours said, to a man,
'That boy will never be one of us,
    Though he does what he blessed well can.'

He went round to all the people
  A paper crown on his head.
Here is some bread from my father.
  Take, eat, he said.

Nobody seemed very hungry.
  Nobody seemed to care.
Nobody saw the god in himself
  Quietly standing there.

He finished up in the papers.
  He came to a very bad end.
He was charged with bringing the living to life.
  No man was that prisoner's friend.

There's only one kind of punishment
  To fit that kind of a crime.
They rigged a trial and shot him dead.
  They were only just in time.

They lifted the young man by the leg,
  They lifted him by the arm,
They locked him in a cathedral
  In case he came to harm.

They stored him safe as water
  Under seven rocks.
One Sunday morning he burst out
  Like a jack-in-the-box.

Through the town he went walking.
  He showed them the holes in his head.
Now do you want any loaves? he cried.
  'Not today,' they said.

CHARLES CAUSLEY

The Land of Counterpane

When I was sick and lay a-bed,
I had two pillows at my head,
And all my toys beside me lay
To keep me happy all the day.

And sometimes for an hour or so
I watched my leaden soldiers go,
With different uniforms and drills,
Among the bed-clothes, through the hills;

And sometimes sent my ships in fleets
All up and down among the sheets;
Or brought my trees and houses out,
And planted cities all about.

I was the giant great and still
That sits upon the pillow-hill,
And sees before him, dale and plain,
The pleasant land of counterpane.

ROBERT LOUIS STEVENSON

A Boy's Head

In it there is a space-ship
and a project
for doing away with piano lessons.

And there is
Noah's ark,
which shall be first.

And there is
an entirely new bird,
an entirely new hare,
an entirely new bumble-bee.

There is a river
that flows upwards.

There is a multiplication table.
There is anti-matter.
And it just cannot be trimmed.

I believe
that only what cannot be trimmed
is a head.

There is much promise
in the circumstance
that so many people have heads.

MIROSLAV HOLUB
translated by Ian Milner

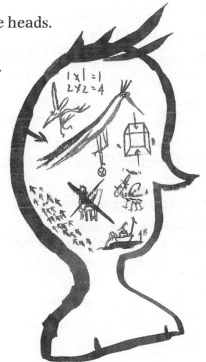

Godolphin Horne
Who was Cursed with the Sin of Pride, and Became a Boot-Black

Godolphin Horne was Nobly Born;
He held the Human Race in Scorn,
And lived with all his Sisters where
His Father lived, in Berkeley Square.
And oh! the Lad was Deathly Proud!
He never shook your Hand or Bowed,
But merely smirked and nodded thus:
How perfectly ridiculous!
Alas! That such Affected Tricks
Should flourish in a Child of Six!
(For such was Young Godolphin's age).
Just then, the Court required a Page,
Whereat the Lord High Chamberlain
(The Kindest and the Best of Men),
He went good-naturedly and took
A Perfectly Enormous Book
Called *People Qualified to Be*
Attendant on His Majesty,
And murmured, as he scanned the list
(To see that no one should be missed),
'There's William Coutts has got the Flu,
And Billy Higgs would never do,
And Guy de Vere is far too young,
And . . . wasn't D'Alton's Father hung?
And as for Alexander Byng! – . . .
I think I know the kind of thing,
A Churchman, cleanly, nobly born,
Come let us say Godolphin Horne?'
But hardly had he said the word

When Murmurs of Dissent were heard.
The King of Iceland's Eldest Son
Said, 'Thank you! I am taking none!'
The Aged Duchess of Athlone
Remarked, in her sub-acid tone,
'I doubt if He is what we need!'
With which the Bishops all agreed;
And even Lady Mary Flood
(So Kind, and oh! so *really* good)
Said, 'No! He wouldn't do at all,
He'd make us feel a lot too small.'
The Chamberlain said, '. . . Well, well, well!
No doubt you're right . . . One cannot tell!'
He took his Gold and Diamond Pen
And Scratched Godolphin out again.
So now Godolphin is the Boy
Who blacks the Boots at the Savoy.

HILAIRE BELLOC

Queens

A cold, bored Queen lived in a castle.
She was Queen as far as the castle walls,
no farther.
Rooks flapped about. HM stared out from the East tower
in her blue robes, in the dull old gold of her crown;
a thin white Queen with grey-green eyes under a tight frown.

She wrote to a second Queen; she penned a formal letter
with a clammy candlewax seal. *I hope
you are feeling better. Please come.*
For three days, a man on a black horse

rode uphill with the letter.
For two days he rode downhill with the answer.
Very well. Very well.
A trembling royal hand reached out, tugged
at the hanging rope of the servants' bell.

Queen Two was fat, with a loud voice
and a temper.
She dressed in a piccalilli yellow.
Queen One came down to greet her
in the Great Pink Hall for dinner.
Clear soup. Spinach. Fish.
What's this? the big Queen bellowed,
Rubbish to make me thinner?
Where is the curry, the pepper, the pickle,
the onion, the mustard and chilli?
Where is the garlic bread?
I'm off to bed.

At daybreak, a quiet Queen sat by her chessboard,
pale, apprehensive, fainter of heart.
A cross Queen thumped in, unthin.
What's going on? Where are the boxing-gloves,
the duelling swords, the snooker cues, where are the darts?
The rooks outside were alarmed, cawed back
at her deafening shout –
I'M GOING OUT!

That night, Queen One mooted a walk
in the castle grounds.
It was mild. There was a moon up above
and a moon in the moat.
They could stroll, calm, polite, Queen hand in Queen glove,
under the yews, the ancient oaks.

Is this a joke? Queen Two snapped.
Where are the bagpipes, the fiddlers three,
where is the karaoke? Answer me that!
TAXI!

So both Queens tried harder, harder.
Queen Thin let Queen Fat
raid the royal larder.
Fat held Thin's wool,
her big, plump, soft regal hands
frozen mid-clap.
Queen Thin knitted away, click, click-clack,
   click-clack.
Then both queens sat in a marble bath –
Fat at the bottom, Thin by the taps –
We are clean Queens, they sang
We are fragrant.
We are very very very clean Queens.

And when it was time,
Queen One managed a slight bow of the head,
Queen Two shuffled the start of a curtsy
under her dress.
Farewell, farewell,
a fat Queen called from a gold coach,
trotting away down the gravel drive, over the moat,
a big puce Queen
with a string of rubies at her throat.
Goodbye, goodbye

Goodbye. A thin Queen waved from a window, shyly,
then fingered her new pearls.
One two three four five six seven.
Seven rooks round a castle started to cry.

CAROL ANN DUFFY

The Twa Corbies

As I was walking all alane,
I heard twa corbies making a mane;
The tane unto the t'other say,
'Where sall we gang and dine to-day?'

'In behint yon auld fail dike,
I wot there lies a new slain knight;
And naebody kens that he lies there,
But his hawk, his hound, and lady fair.

'His hound is to the hunting gane,
His hawk to fetch the wild-fowl hame,
His lady's ta'en another mate,
So we may mak our dinner sweet.

'Ye'll sit on his white hause-bane,
And I'll pike out his bonny blue een;
Wi' ae lock o' his gowden hair
We'll theek our nest when it grows bare.

'Mony a one for him makes mane,
But nane sall ken where he is gane;
O'er his white banes, when they are bare,
The wind sall blaw for evermair.'

ANONYMOUS

Windy Nights

Whenever the moon and stars are set,
    Whenever the wind is high,
All night long in the dark and wet,
    A man goes riding by.
Late in the night when the fires are out,
Why does he gallop and gallop about?

Whenever the trees are crying aloud,
    And ships are tossed at sea,
By, on the highway, low and loud,
    By at the gallop goes he.
By at the gallop he goes, and then
By he comes back at the gallop again.

ROBERT LOUIS STEVENSON

[117]

In the Formal Garden

A peacock feather. And a simple stone
in the herbaceous border like a child's
first tooth, carved *BENJIE.*
EVER FAITHFUL. 1899.

And I've been here before.
A gust of dead leaves brushes by
like bustled skirts. I step aside; I know
my place: the gardener's boy

who crouches by the trellis, there,
to glimpse three lacy Misses flit and chime,
their shuttlecock hung motionless
above their heads, like time.

A spaniel pup flop-lollops at their heels.
Then that dry rustling: Lady M.
stands over me . . . Pa wrings his cap and begs:
'He's not a *bad* boy, ma'am.'

She freezes: 'If I ever catch him
looking at my gels again . . .' Unmanned,
bowed, slashing weeds, I catch the hush
of silks, and round, my billhook in my hand,

on a pinched proud face, beneath
its silly coronet. Waddling in draggled finery,
the peacock stares. It rattles up its fan
in a shivering hiss. And screams.

The sky is darkening fast. 'Get in,'
Pa calls. 'Daft ha'p'orth.' From the shed
we hear it shriek again. Pa grins,
'Like the voice of the dead!

Damned bird. I'd wring its neck.'
The first drops streak the pane.
Somewhere, a yappity panic breaks and falls
to whimpers: Benjie, left out in the rain . . .

PHILIP GROSS

The Long-Haired Boy

There was a boy in our town with long hair –
I mean really long hair –
And everybody pointed at him
And laughed at him
And made fun of him.
And when he walked down the street
The people would roar
And stick their tongues out
And make funny faces
And run in and slam their door
And shout at him from the window
Until he couldn't stand it anymore.
So he sat down and cried
Till his whole body shook
And pretty soon his hair shook too,
And it flapped
And flapped –
And he lifted –
And flew –
Straight up in the air like a helicopter.
Jenny Ricks saw him and dropped her
Knitting and screamed, 'It's a flying kid!'
Lukey Hastings ran and hid
Under Old Man Merrill's car,

Miss Terance fainted, Henry Quist
Tried to shoot him down, but missed –
'I thought he was a crow,' he said.
And 'round he sailed all through the day,
Smiling in the strangest way,
With the wind in his hair
And the sun in his eyes.
We saw him swoop and bank and rise.
He brushed the treetops
And skimmed the grass
On Yerbey's lawn and almost crashed
Right into Hansen's silo – but
Zoomed up in time and almost hit
The courthouse. Old Man Cooley bit
Right through his napkin when he saw
A kid fly through the diner door –
And out of the window, tipping the ladder –
Where Smokey was painting, he almost had a

Heart attack – he clung to a rafter.
The kid flew on –
Us runnin' after,
Cheering and sweating
And screaming, 'Hooray!'
Major Lowry shouted, 'Hey –
Come down here, kid. We'd like to say
How proud of you we are today.
Who ever thought our little
Town would have a hero in it?
So I'd like to proclaim this day – hey, kid!
Will you please come down for just a minute?'
But the flying kid did not come down.
He treaded air above the town,
Sort of cryin' and looking down
At all of us here on the ground.
Then up he flew, up into the clouds,
Flapping and flying so far and high.
Out past the hills and into the sky
Until a tiny speck against the sun
Was all we could see of him . . . then he was gone.

SHEL SILVERSTEIN

On the Ning Nang Nong

On the Ning Nang Nong
Where the Cows go Bong!
And the Monkeys all say Boo!
There's a Nong Nang Ning
Where the trees go Ping!
And the tea pots Jibber Jabber Joo.
On the Nong Ning Nang
All the mice go Clang!
And you just can't catch 'em when they do!
So it's Ning Nang Nong!
Cows go Bong!
Nong Nang Ning!
Trees go Ping!
Nong Ning Nang!
The mice go Clang!
What a noisy place to belong,
Is the Ning Nang Ning Nang Nong!!

SPIKE MILLIGAN

The Owl and the Pussy-cat

The Owl and the Pussy-cat went to sea
    In a beautiful pea-green boat,
They took some honey, and plenty of money,
    Wrapped up in a five-pound note.
The Owl looked up to the stars above,

And sang to a small guitar,
'O lovely Pussy! O Pussy, my love,
  What a beautiful Pussy you are,
      You are,
      You are!
What a beautiful Pussy you are!'

Pussy said to the Owl, 'You elegant fowl!
  How charmingly sweet you sing!
O let us be married! too long we have tarried:
  But what shall we do for a ring?'
They sailed away, for a year and a day,
  To the land where the Bong-tree grows
And there in a wood a Piggy-wig stood
  With a ring at the end of his nose,
      His nose,
      His nose,
  With a ring at the end of his nose.

'Dear Pig, are you willing to sell for one shilling
    Your ring?' Said the Piggy, 'I will.'
So they took it away, and were married next day
    By the Turkey who lives on the hill.
They dined on mince, and slices of quince,
    Which they ate with a runcible spoon;
And hand in hand, on the edge of the sand,
    They danced by the light of the moon,
            The moon,
            The moon,
    They danced by the light of the moon.

EDWARD LEAR

Stocking and Shirt

Stocking and shirt
    Can trip and prance,
Though nobody's in them
    To make them dance.
See how they waltz
    Or minuet,
Watch the petticoat
    Pirouette.
This is the dance
    Of stocking and shirt,
When the wind puts on
    The white lace skirt.
Old clothes and young clothes
    Dance together,
Twirling and whirling
    In the mad March weather.

'Come!' cries the wind,
  To stocking and shirt.
'Away!' cries the wind
  To blouse and skirt.
Then clothes and wind
  All pull together,
Tugging like mad
  In the mad March weather.
Across the garden
  They suddenly fly
And over the far hedge
  High, high, high!
'Stop!' cries the housewife,
  But all too late,
Her clothes have passed
  The furthest gate.
They are gone for ever
  In the bright blue sky,
And only the handkerchiefs
  Wave good-bye.

JAMES REEVES

Pride

Two birds sat in a big white bra
  That swung as it hung
  On the washing-line.

They sang: 'Hurray!' and they sang: 'Hurrah!
Of all the birds we're the best by far!
Our hammock swings to the highest star!
  No life like yours and mine!'

They were overheard
   By a third
   Bird

That swooped down on to a nearby tree
And sneered: 'Knickers! It's plain to see
A bird in a tree is worth two in a bra.
   There's no bird *half* so fine!'

And it seemed indeed that he was right
For the washing-line was *far* too tight
And old and frayed. As the laundry flapped,
The big wind heaved and the rope . . . *snapped!*

You should have heard
   The third
   Bird.

He cried: 'Aha!
For all their chatter and la-de-dah,
They didn't get far in their Big White Bra!
If there *is* a bird who's a Superstar,
It's me, it's me, it's me!'

Down to the ground
He dived in his glee

And the Big Black Cat
Enjoyed his tea.

   KIT WRIGHT

The Carrion Crow

A carrion crow sat on an oak
And watched where the line of battle broke.

A carrion crow sat on an ash –
He heard the spears' and shields' clash.

A carrion crow sat on a pine:
The long-bows are bent, the swift arrows whine.

A carrion crow sat on an elm:
The broad sword batters the bright-plumed helm.

A carrion crow sat on a yew:
On Bosworth Field lies a crimson dew.

A carrion crow sat on a thorn,
Where the crown of England had rolled, forlorn.

JOHN HEATH-STUBBS

I Saw a Jolly Hunter

I saw a jolly hunter
    With a jolly gun
Walking in the country
    In the jolly sun

In the jolly meadow
    Sat a jolly hare.
Saw the jolly hunter.
    Took jolly care.

Hunter jolly eager –
    Sight of jolly prey.
Forgot gun pointing
    Wrong jolly way.

Jolly hunter jolly head
    Over heels gone.
Jolly old safety catch
    Not jolly on.

Bang went the jolly gun.
    Hunter jolly dead.
Jolly hare got clean away.
    Jolly good, I said.

CHARLES CAUSLEY

To a Squirrel at Kyle-na-no

Come play with me;
Why should you run
Through the shaking tree
As though I'd a gun
To strike you dead?
When all I would do
Is to scratch your head
And let you go.

W. B. YEATS

The Law of the Jungle

Now this is the Law of the Jungle – as old and as true as the sky;
And the Wolf that shall keep it may prosper, but the Wolf that shall
  break it must die.

As the creeper that girdles the tree-trunk the Law runneth forward
  and back –
For the strength of the Pack is the Wolf, and the strength of the Wolf is
  the Pack.

Wash daily from nose-tip to tail-tip; drink deeply, but never too
  deep;
And remember the night is for hunting, and forget not the day is
  for sleep.

The Jackal may follow the Tiger, but, Cub, when thy whiskers
  are grown,
Remember the Wolf is a hunter – go forth and get food of thine
  own.

Keep peace with the Lords of the Jungle – the Tiger, the Panther,
  the Bear;
And trouble not Hathi the Silent, and mock not the Boar in his
  lair.

When Pack meets with Pack in the Jungle, and neither will go
  from the trail,
Lie down till the leaders have spoken – it may be fair words shall
  prevail.

When ye fight with a Wolf of the Pack, ye must fight him alone
  and afar,
Lest others take part in the quarrel, and the Pack be diminished
  by war.

The Lair of the Wolf is his refuge, and where he has made him his
   home,
Not even the Head Wolf may enter, not even the Council may
   come.

The Lair of the Wolf is his refuge, but where he has digged it too
   plain,
The Council shall send him a message, and so he shall change it
   again.

If ye kill before midnight, be silent, and wake not the woods with
   your bay,
Lest ye frighten the deer from the crops, and the brothers go
   empty away.

Ye may kill for yourselves, and your mates, and your cubs as
   they need, and ye can;
But kill not for pleasure of killing, and *seven times never kill Man!*

If ye plunder his Kill from a weaker, devour not all in thy pride;
Pack-Right is the right of the meanest; so leave him the head and
   the hide.

The Kill of the Pack is the meat of the Pack. Ye must eat where it
   lies;
And no one may carry away of that meat to his lair, or he dies.

The Kill of the Wolf is the meat of the Wolf. He may do what he
   will,
But, till he has given permission, the Pack may not eat of that
   Kill.

Cub-Right is the right of the Yearling. From all of his Pack he
   may claim
Full-gorge when the killer has eaten; and none may refuse him
   the same.

Lair-Right is the right of the Mother. From all of her year she may claim
One haunch of each kill for her litter; and none may deny her the same.

Cave-Right is the right of the Father – to hunt by himself for his own:
He is freed of all calls to the Pack; he is judged by the Council alone.

Because of his age and his cunning, because of his gripe and his paw,
In all that the Law leaveth open, the word of the Head Wolf is Law.

Now these are the Laws of the Jungle, and many and mighty are they;
But the head and the hoof of the Law and the haunch and the hump is –
Obey!

RUDYARD KIPLING

A Boy in a Snow Shower

Said the first snowflake
No, I'm not a shilling,
I go quicker than a white butterfly in summer.

Said the second snowflake
Be patient, boy.
Seize me, I'm a drop of water on the end of your finger.

The third snowflake said,
A star?
No, I've drifted down out of that big blue-black cloud.

And the fourth snowflake,
Ah good, the road
Is hard as flint, it tolls like iron under your boots.

And the fifth snowflake,
Go inside, boy,
Fetch your scarf, a bonnet, the sledge.

The sixth snowflake sang,
I'm a city of sixes,
Crystal hexagons, a hushed sextet.

And the trillionth snowflake,
All ends with me –
I and my brother Fire, we end all.

GEORGE MACKAY BROWN

Hunters in the Snow
(A detail from the painting by Bruegel)

This is the agreement:
I pull you to your house
and you pull me to mine – OK?
Whoever is pulling has to make sure
that we don't slide
on any weak spots in the ice
and the horse has to trot a little
because it's not such fun
if you're riding on a sled
and the horse is just walking
all the time – is it?
The horse can have only one
resting stop and shouldn't spend

the whole trip moaning
about how slippery the ice is
and how heavy the passenger is.
If the horse goes over a bumpy area
and the sled capsizes
the passenger gets another ride free
to wherever she wants to go.
Since I thought up all the rules,
I will be the first-ever passenger.
You can start acting like a nag now.

JULIE O'CALLAGHAN

The Leader

I wanna be the leader
I wanna be the leader
Can I be the leader?
Can I? I can?
Promise? Promise?
Yippee, I'm the leader
I'm the leader

OK what shall we do?

ROGER MCGOUGH

Dumb Insolence

I'm big for ten years old
Maybe that's why they get at me

Teachers, parents, cops
Always getting at me

When they get at me

I don't hit em
They can do you for that

I don't swear at em
They can do you for that

I stick my hands in my pockets
And stare at them

And while I stare at them
I think about sick

They call it dumb insolence

They don't like it
But they can't do you for it

ADRIAN MITCHELL

The Blackboard

Five foot by five foot
(The smalls have measured it).
Smooth black surface
(Wiped by a small after every class).
Five different colours of chalk
And a class of twenty-five smalls,
One big.

Does the big break up the chalk
Into twenty-five or twenty-six
And invite the smalls to make
A firework show of colours
Shapes and words

[134]

Starting on the blackboard
But soon overflowing
   All over the room
      All over the school
        All over the town
          All over the country
            All over the world?

    No.

The big looks at the textbook
Which was written by a big
And published by a firm of bigs
The textbook says
The names and dates of Nelson's battles.
So the big writes, in white,
Upon the black of the blackboard,
The names and dates of Nelson's battles.
The smalls copy into their books
The names and dates of Nelson's battles.

     Nelson was a big
Who died fighting for freedom or something.

ADRIAN MITCHELL

Kidnapped

This morning I got kidnapped
By three masked men.
They stopped me on the sidewalk,
And offered me some candy,
And when I wouldn't take it
They grabbed me by the collar,

And pinned my arms behind me,
And shoved me in the backseat
Of this big black limousine and
Tied my hands behind my back
With sharp and rusty wire.
Then they put a blindfold on me
So I couldn't see where they took me,
And plugged up my ears with cotton
So I couldn't hear their voices.
And drove for 20 miles or
At least for 20 minutes, and then
Dragged me from the car down to
Some cold and moldy basement,
Where they stuck me in a corner
And went off to get the ransom
Leaving one of them to guard me
With a shotgun pointed at me,
Tied up sitting on a stool . . .
That's why I'm late for school!

SHEL SILVERSTEIN

Matilda
Who Told Lies, and was Burned to Death

Matilda told such Dreadful Lies,
It made one Gasp and Stretch one's Eyes;
Her Aunt, who, from her Earliest Youth,
Had kept a Strict Regard for Truth,
Attempted to Believe Matilda:
The effort very nearly killed her,
And would have done so, had not She
Discovered this Infirmity.

For once, towards the Close of Day,
Matilda, growing tired of play,
And finding she was left alone,
Went tiptoe to the Telephone
And summoned the Immediate Aid
Of London's Noble Fire-Brigade.
Within an hour the Gallant Band
Were pouring in on every hand,
From Putney, Hackney Downs, and Bow
With Courage high and Hearts a-glow
They galloped, roaring through the Town,
'Matilda's House is Burning Down!'
Inspired by British Cheers and Loud
Proceeding from the Frenzied Crowd,
They ran their ladders through a score
Of windows on the Ball Room Floor;
And took Peculiar Pains to Souse
The Pictures up and down the House,
Until Matilda's Aunt succeeded
In showing them they were not needed;
And even then she had to pay
To get the Men to go away!

It happened that a few Weeks later
Her Aunt was off to the Theatre
To see that Interesting Play
The Second Mrs Tanqueray.
She had refused to take her Niece
To hear this Entertaining Piece:
A Deprivation Just and Wise
To Punish her for Telling Lies.
That Night a Fire *did* break out –
You should have heard Matilda Shout!
You should have heard her Scream and Bawl,

And throw the window up and call
To People passing in the Street –
(The rapidly increasing Heat
Encouraging her to obtain
Their confidence) – but all in vain!
For every time She shouted 'Fire!'
They only answered 'Little Liar'!
And therefore when her Aunt returned,
Matilda, and the House, were Burned.

HILAIRE BELLOC

The Boy who Laughed at Santa Claus

In Baltimore there lived a boy.
He wasn't anybody's joy.
Although his name was Jabez Dawes
His character was full of flaws.
In school he never led his classes,
He hid old ladies' reading glasses,
His mouth was open when he chewed,
And elbows to the table glued.
He stole the milk of hungry kittens,
And walked through doors marked NO ADMITTANCE.
He said he acted thus because
There wasn't any Santa Claus.
Another trick that tickled Jabez
Was crying 'Boo!' at little babies.
He brushed his teeth, they said in town,
Sideways instead of up and down.

Yet people pardoned every sin,
And viewed his antics with a grin,
Till they were told by Jabez Dawes,
'There isn't any Santa Claus!'
Deploring how he did behave,
His parents swiftly sought their grave.
They hurried through the portals pearly,
And Jabez left the funeral early.

Like whooping cough, from child to child,
He sped to spread the rumor wild:
'Sure as my name is Jabez Dawes
There isn't any Santa Claus!'
Slunk like a weasel or a marten
Through nursery and kindergarten,

Whispering low to every tot,
'There isn't any, no there's not!'

The children wept all Christmas eve
And Jabez chortled up his sleeve.
No infant dared hang up his stocking
For fear of Jabez' ribald mocking.
He sprawled on his untidy bed,
Fresh malice dancing in his head,
When presently with scalp-a-tingling,
Jabez heard a distant jingling;
He heard the crunch of sleigh and hoof
Crisply alighting on the roof.

What good to rise and bar the door?
A shower of soot was on the floor,
What was beheld by Jabez Dawes?
The fireplace full of Santa Claus!
Then Jabez fell upon his knees
With cries of 'Don't,' and 'Pretty please.'
He howled, 'I don't know where you read it,
But anyhow, I never said it!'

'Jabez,' replied the angry saint,
'It isn't I, it's you that ain't.
Although there is a Santa Claus,
There isn't any Jabez Dawes!'
Said Jabez then with impudent vim,
'Oh, yes there is, and I am him!
Your magic don't scare me, it doesn't' –
And suddenly he found he wasn't!

From grimy feet to grimy locks,
Jabez became a Jack-in-the-box,
An ugly toy with springs unsprung,

Forever sticking out his tongue.
The neighbors heard his mournful squeal;
They searched for him, but not with zeal.

No trace was found of Jabez Dawes,
Which led to thunderous applause,
And people drank a loving cup
And went and hung their stockings up.

All you who sneer at Santa Claus,
Beware the fate of Jabez Dawes,
The saucy boy who mocked the saint.
Donner and Blitzen licked off his paint.

OGDEN NASH

Miss Strawberry

I   HER PURSE

Miss Strawberry has a long fat purse
To keep her money in.
It is a rare and handsome purse
Made of crocodile skin.
It is crocodile skin without a doubt
For she did not take the crocodile out
And when she walks to town to shop
He follows behind her clop, clop-clop,
And opens his mouth and bellows aloud
And swishes his tail amongst the crowd.
Now and again there's an angry mutter
As a man is swept into the gutter.
When in a shop it is time to pay
Shopkeepers look at the brute in dismay

When Miss Strawberry says, 'Crocky, open wide,'
And, 'Shopman, your money is deep inside.
Just dodge the slashing of his paws
And reach beyond those ugly jaws;
But I warn you if you make him cough
He'll probably bite your arm right off.'
The shopkeeper usually says, 'No worry.
Pay next month. I'm in no hurry.'
But a grocer once, owed four-pounds-ten,
Said, 'That's worth more than one of my men.'
He called his errand-boy, 'Hey son,
Come over here, we'll have some fun.
I'll hold your legs and guard you while
You crawl in this quiet old crocodile
And collect in his vitals four-pounds-ten.
If you bring it out again
I'll give you sixpence for your trouble.
Come here, son, and at the double!'
Now the length of Miss Strawberry's crocodile's throat
Is four times as long as a shopkeeper's coat.
The crocodile opened fearfully wide
And the errand-boy crawled right down inside.
When he had gathered four-pounds-ten
And hurriedly tried to back out again,
The crocodile closed his jaws with a smile,
Saying, 'One of the joys of a crocodile,
Indeed you might say, his favourite joy,
Is making a meal of a messenger-boy.'

4   HER PIG

Miss Strawberry's pig
Has grown too big

And this is breakfast only:
Two bags of oats, two bags of wheat,
A swineherd slow upon his feet:
And that was breakfast only.

Miss Strawberry's pig
Has grown too big
And this is luncheon only:
All the bedding in his sty,
The remains of last week's pumpkin pie,
A bushel of peas, a bag of bones –
Known to some as Mrs Jones –
And that was luncheon only.

Miss Strawberry's pig
Has grown too big
And this is dinner only:
A ton of corn, a ton of chaff.
He gobbles this in an hour and a half
Then he angrily charges his pen
Squealing, 'It's breakfast time again':
And that was dinner only.

ERIC ROLLS

The Sea

The sea is a hungry dog,
Giant and grey.
He rolls on the beach all day.
With his clashing teeth and shaggy jaws
Hour upon hour he gnaws
The rumbling, tumbling stones,
And 'Bones, bones, bones, bones!'

The giant sea-dog moans,
Licking his greasy paws.

And when the night wind roars
And the moon rocks in the stormy cloud,
He bounds to his feet and snuffs and sniffs,
Shaking his wet sides over the cliffs,
And howls and hollos long and loud.

But on quiet days in May or June,
When even the grasses on the dune
Play no more their reedy tune,
With his head between his paws
He lies on the sandy shores,
So quiet, so quiet, he scarcely snores.

JAMES REEVES

The Old Ships

I have seen old ships sail like swans asleep
Beyond the village which men still call Tyre,
With leaden age o'ercargoed, dipping deep
For Famagusta and the hidden sun
That rings black Cyprus with a lake of fire;
And all those ships were certainly so old
Who knows how oft with squat and noisy gun,
Questing brown slaves or Syrian oranges,
The pirate Genoese
Hell-raked them till they rolled
Blood, water, fruit and corpses up the hold.
But now through friendly seas they softly run,
Painted the mid-sea blue or shore-sea green,
Still patterned with the vine and grapes in gold.

But I have seen,
Pointing her shapely shadows from the dawn
And image tumbled on a rose-swept bay,
A drowsy ship of some yet older day;
And, wonder's breath indrawn,
Thought I – who knows – who knows – but in that same
(Fished up beyond Ææa, patched up new
– Stern painted brighter blue –)
That talkative, bald-headed seaman came
(Twelve patient comrades sweating at the oar)
From Troy's doom-crimson shore,
And with great lies about his wooden horse
Set the crew laughing, and forgot his course.

It was so old a ship – who knows, who knows?
– And yet so beautiful, I watched in vain
To see the mast burst open with a rose,
And the whole deck put on its leaves again.

J. E. FLECKER

In Goes Robin

In goes Robin, bold as brass,
Into all that moving mass
Of blue and green and creamy foam
Just as though he were at home.
Water doesn't frighten him,
He will sink till he can swim,
When a big wave knocks him down
Up will come his laughing brown
Spluttering face. He has no fear,
The sea is his: yes, all that clear
Stretch of water, touching all
The shores of earth, that makes its call
On English cliffs and Indian sands,
And coral isles and mountain-lands,
And crowded ports and lonely bays:
His, should he choose to go those ways,
With all the ships that sail on it,
And all the gulls and mews that flit,
And all the fishes in the blue,
And all the wrecks and icebergs too.
The sea was Robin's from the first,
He saw it and was all athirst,
He couldn't *wait* to reach it – whether
Its waves were tumbled all together,
Or it was bright and smooth as glass,
In went Robin, bold as brass.

ELEANOR FARJEON

The River in March

Now the river is rich, but her voice is low.
It is her Mighty Majesty the sea
Travelling among the villages incognito.

Now the river is poor. No song, just a thin mad whisper.
The winter floods have ruined her.
She squats between draggled banks, fingering her rags and
    rubbish.

And now the river is rich. A deep choir.
It is the lofty clouds, that work in heaven,
Going on their holiday to the sea.

The river is poor again. All her bones are showing.
Through a dry wig of bleached flotsam she peers up ashamed
From her slum of sticks.

Now the river is rich, collecting shawls and minerals.
Rain brought fatness, but she takes ninety-nine percent
Leaving the fields just one percent to survive on.

And now she is poor. Now she is East wind sick.
She huddles in holes and corners. The brassy sun gives her a
    headache.
She has lost all her fish. And she shivers.

But now once more she is rich. She is viewing her lands.
A hoard of king-cups spills from her folds, it blazes, it cannot be
    hidden.
A salmon, a sow of solid silver,

Bulges to glimpse it.

TED HUGHES

Don't Call Alligator Long-Mouth till You Cross River

Call alligator long-mouth
call alligator saw-mouth
call alligator pushy-mouth
call alligator scissors-mouth
call alligator raggedy-mouth
call alligator bumpy-bum
call alligator all dem rude word
but better wait
           till you cross river.

JOHN AGARD

Sardines

A baby Sardine
Saw her first submarine:
She was scared and watched through a peephole.

'Oh, come, come, come,'
Said the Sardine's mum,
'It's only a tin full of people.'

SPIKE MILLIGAN

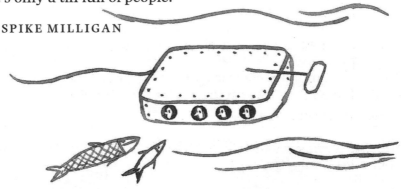

Let's Hear it for the Limpet

If there's one animal that isn't a wimp, it
Is the limpet.

Let me provide an explanation
For my admiration.

To start with, it's got two thousand tiny teeth
Beneath

Its comical conical-hat-shaped, greeny-grey shell:
A tongue as well

That rasps the delicate seaweed through its front door:
What's more –

And this is what gives me the greatest surprise –
Two bright eyes

Indoors at the end of long tentacles poking out, which
Twitch.

But its funniest feature by far is its foot
That's put

Straight down to clamp it fast to the rock.
(Gulls knock,

You see, at the shell to try and winkle it off
For scoff.)

But the limpet does more with its foot than Ian Rush.
Forsaking the crush

Of its home life it stomps off, foraging, humping its shell with it,
Then thinks, 'The hell with it,'

And slithers back to exactly where it began.
What a man

Is the limpet, in his wilderness of weed!

Needless to say, they make very good pets indeed.

KIT WRIGHT

A Colossal Glossary

The **aardvark's** a kind of ant-eater, an 'earth-pig' in Dutch,
while **abracadabra** is a charm much

favoured by alchemists.
As for that wine-coloured gem, the **amethyst,**

A Greek would place it in his cup 'so as not to be drunk',
a thought no foul-mouthed **Anglo-Saxon** ever thunk.

Azure is the blue of lapis lazuli.
The **bandicoot** is a rat from Australasia

that likes to **browse** or graze on the tender shoots of rice.
A **carbon-copy**'s a replica, though only once or twice.

Yellow or green, **chartreuse** is a liqueur
distilled, as always, by monks. The **coypu**'s prized for its fur;

not so the wild dog or **dingo.**
An **eland**'s an African antelope. In medical lingo

an **epiglottis** is a tongue, an **esophagus** a gizzard.
A **glitch** would be a snag or hazard.

The **ibex** is a mountain goat; **i.e.** is short for **id est,**
in Latin 'that is'. A pain in the side

was once a **jade,** a word which
we now use of the greenish stone deemed to mend the stitch.

A **jennet** might also be a jade, in the horse-sense.
Soldiers in **khaki** uniforms tense

when they hear the siren-song of a **klaxon,**
since it almost always represents a call to action.

A **lagoon** is a shallow lake, usually on the coast.
The nocturnal **lemur** is essentially a ghost.

A **Lilo** is a rubber raft, while a **limousine**
is a vehicle whose occupants thankfully can't be seen

since they're often types who say **moi** for 'me'
and have a penchant for drinking sparkling **mongoose**-pee.

Whipped cream is the main ingredient of **mousse.**
The **narwhal** relies on its tusk when hunting Eskimos.

Nebuchadnezzar was the king of Babylon
for whom the writing on the wall was plain

as plain can be; a **nicety** may be either a subtle
or idle distinction: as such, it's its own rebuttal.

The **oryx,** like all gazelles, is thought by lions to wallow
in self-pity. An **osier** is a type of willow.

A **pickle** is anything preserved in vinegar or brine.
As one pine opined to another pitch-pine,

'He that toucheth pitch shall be defiled';
though **pitch** more commonly refers to asphalt.

The root of **prehensile** is 'prehendere', to seize;
you may already have grasped that a **quagga** is a wild ass.

The **rouble** and **rupee** are Russian and Indian coins.
To be **scrupulous** is to have qualms of conscience,

from 'scrupulus', a stone with a cutting edge;
the reed with a razor-sharp blade is **sedge**.

Tamburlaine, also known as Tamerlane or Timur,
was a Mongol king whose deportment was anything but
   demure,

his stock-in-trade being rapine and reprisal.
The **tapir** lives as a hermit in the rain-forests of Brazil

where it meditates on **Theology**;
'In the beginning was the Word, and the Word was Algae'.

A no less avid theologian was Thomas de **Torquemada**
whose cruel streak ran the gamut

from burning at the stake through hanging by a gaff
to the flaying of some fatted divinity calf

all in the name of Truth and Justice.
On the subject of the 'thrice-great' Hermes **Trismegistus**,

or his Lord Lieutenant, Zoroaster,
my lips are sealed. I will say this; a **trundle** is a caster.

Often mistaken for a llama or alpaca, the newly-shorn **vicuña**
spits at the thought of the Norseman or **Viking**

who stole the shirt off his back. The chief
sense of **winnow** is to fan, to separate the wheat from the chaff,

the sheep from the goats, good from evil.
It's hard to categorize the **xylophagan**, this wood-boring weevil

makes of something nothing, **zilch**;
just as a worm may contain an armada, little much,

so the meanings of all the rest
of the words in this book are buried in one, a treasurechest.

PAUL MULDOON

The Visitor

A crumbling churchyard, the sea and the moon;
The waves had gouged out grave and bone;
A man was walking, late and alone . . .

He saw a skeleton on the ground;
A ring on a bony hand he found.

He ran home to his wife and gave her the ring.
'Oh, where did you get it?' He said not a thing.

'It's the loveliest ring in the world,' she said.
As it glowed on her finger. They skipped off to bed.

At midnight they woke. In the dark outside,
'Give me my ring!' a chill voice cried.

'What was that, William? What did it say?'
'Don't worry, my dear. It'll soon go away.'

'I'm coming!' A skeleton opened the door.
'Give me my ring!' It was crossing the floor.

'What was that, William? What did it say?'
'Don't worry, my dear. It'll soon go away.'

'I'm reaching you now! I'm climbing the bed.'
The wife pulled the sheet right over her head.

It was torn from her grasp and tossed in the air:
'I'll drag you out of bed by the hair!'

'What was that, William? What did it say?'
'Throw the ring through the window! THROW IT AWAY!'

She threw it. The skeleton leapt from the sill,
Scooped up the ring and clattered downhill,
Fainter . . . and fainter . . . Then all was still.

IAN SERRAILLIER

The Angel

She looked over her shoulder –
Nobody was near,
The clouds seemed deserted,
The coast seemed clear,
So the angel up in heaven
Undid her shining wings
And shrugged them off: nasty
Heavy old things.

She leapt – she vaulted –
Cartwheeled – somersaulted –
Back-flipped – landed –
Sprang – hand-standed –
Gyrated on her halo,
Legs up in the air,
Nightie round her shoulders,
Body all bare.

What was that? A noise,
Something like a cough,
And as no angel's decent
With her white wings off,
She zipped them back and, just in time,

Started praying fast
As, wrapped in all his mystery,
God strolled past.

RICHARD EDWARDS

The Devil

From his brimstone bed at the break of day
A walking the Devil is gone
To visit his snug little farm, the earth
And see how his stock goes on.

Over the hill and over the dale,
And he went over the plain,
And backward and forward he switched his long tail
As a gentleman switches his cane.

And how then was the Devil dressed?
Oh! he was in his Sunday's best:
His jacket was red and his breeches were blue
And there was a hole where the tail came through.

SAMUEL TAYLOR COLERIDGE

The New Vestments

There lived an old man in the Kingdom of Tess,
Who invented a purely original dress;
And when it was perfectly made and complete,
He opened the door, and walked into the street.

[155]

By way of a hat, he'd a loaf of Brown Bread,
In the middle of which he inserted his head; –
His Shirt was made up of no end of dead Mice,
The warmth of whose skins was quite fluffy and nice; –
His Drawers were of Rabbit-skins; – so were his Shoes; –
His Stockings were skins, – but it is not known whose; –
His Waistcoat and Trowsers were made of Pork Chops; –
His Buttons were Jujubes, and Chocolate Drops; –
His Coat was all Pancakes with Jam for a border,
And a girdle of Biscuits to keep it in order;
And he wore over all, as a screen from bad weather,
A Cloak of green Cabbage-leaves stitched all together.

He had walked a short way, when he heard a great noise,
Of all sorts of Beasticles, Birdlings, and Boys; –
And from every long street and dark lane in the town
Beasts, Birdles, and Boys in a tumult rushed down.
Two Cows and a half ate his Cabbage-leaf Cloak; –
Four Apes seized his Girdle, which vanished like smoke; –
Three Kids ate up half of his Pancaky Coat, –
And the tails were devour'd by an ancient He Goat; –

An army of Dogs in a twinkling tore *up* his
Pork Waistcoat and Trowsers to give to their Puppies; –
And while they were growling, and mumbling the Chops,
Ten Boys prigged the Jujubes and Chocolate Drops. –
He tried to run back to his house, but in vain,
For Scores of fat Pigs came again and again; –
They rushed out of stables and hovels and doors, –
They tore off his stockings, his shoes, and his drawers; –
And now from the housetops with screechings descend,
Striped, spotted, white, black, and gray Cats without end,
They jumped on his shoulders and knocked off his hat, –
When Crows, Ducks, and Hens made a mincemeat of that; –
They speedily flew at his sleeves in a trice,
And utterly tore up his Shirt of dead Mice; –
They swallowed the last of his Shirt with a squall, –
Whereon he ran home with no clothes on at all.

And he said to himself as he bolted the door,
'I will not wear a similar dress any more,
'Any more, any more, any more, never more!'

EDWARD LEAR

The Mummy

(*The Mummy* [of Rameses II] *was met at Orly airport by
Mme Saunier-Seïte.* – News item, Sept. 1976)

– May I welcome Your Majesty to Paris.

– Mm.

– I hope the flight from Cairo was reasonable.

– Mmmmm.

– We have a germ-proof room at the Museum of Man
   where we trust Your Majesty will have peace and quiet.

– Unh-unh.

– I am sorry, but this is necessary.
   Your Majesty's person harbours a fungus.

– Fng fng's, hn?

– Well, it is something attacking your cells.
   Your Majesty is gently deteriorating
   after nearly four thousand years
   becalmed in masterly embalmment.
   We wish to save you from the worm.

– Wrm hrm! Mgh-mgh-mgh.

– Indeed I know it must be distressing
   to a pharaoh and a son of Ra,
   to the excavator of Abu Simbel
   that glorious temple in the rock,
   to the perfecter of Karnak hall,
   to the hammer of the Hittites,
   to the colossus whose colossus
   raised in red granite at holy Thebes
   sixteen-men-high astounds the desert
   shattered, as Your Majesty in life
   shattered the kingdom and oppressed the poor
   with such lavish grandeur and panache,
   to Rameses, to Ozymandias,
   to the Louis Quatorze of the Nile,
   how bitter it must be to feel
   a microbe eat your camphored bands.
   But we are here to help Your Majesty.

We shall encourage you to unwind.
You have many useful years ahead.

– M' n'm 'z 'zym'ndias, kng'v kngz!

– Yes yes. Well, Shelley is dead now.
   He was not embalmed. He will not write
   about Your Majesty again.

– T't'nkh'm'n? H'tsh'ps't?
   'khn't'n? N'f'rt'ti? Mm? Mm?

– The hall of fame has many mansions.
   Your Majesty may rest assured
   your deeds will always be remembered.

– Youmm w'm'nn. B't'f'lll w'm'nnnn.
   No w'm'nnn f'r th'zndz y'rz.

– Your Majesty, what are you doing?

– Ng! Mm. Mhm. Mm? Mm? Mmmmm.

– Your Majesty, Your Majesty! You'll break your stitches!

– Fng st'chez fng's wrm hrm.

– I really hate to have to use
   a hypodermic on a mummy,
   but we cannot have you strain yourself.
   Remember your fungus, Your Majesty.

– Fng. Zzzzzzzz.

– That's right.

– Aaaaaaaah.

EDWIN MORGAN

The Little Ghost's Song

I'd like to be human again.
I'd like to get wet in the rain.
I wouldn't mind toothache
Just for living's sake!
I'd like to get wet in the rain.
I'd like to be human again.
I'd like to kick a ball
And my foot not go through at all!
What's the good of being a ghost
If you can't eat jam and toast?
If you can't pull a funny face,
Or be sent to bed in disgrace?
I'd rather be scared than scare,
I'd like to breathe some air.
I'd like to get wet in the rain.
I'd love to be human again!

BRIAN PATTEN

Gust Becos I Cud Not Spel

Gust becos I cud not spel
It did not mean I was daft
When the boys in school red my riting
Some of them laffed

But now I am the dictater
They have to rite like me
Utherwise they cannot pas
Ther GCSE

Some of the girls wer ok
But those who laffed a lot
Have al bean rownded up
And hav recintly bean shot

The teecher who corrected my speling
As not been shot at al
But four the last fifteen howers
As bean standing up against a wal

He has to stand ther until he can spel
Figgymisgrugifooniyn the rite way
I think he will stand ther forever
I just inventid it today

BRIAN PATTEN

First Day at School

A millionbillionwillion miles from home
Waiting for the bell to go. (To go where?)
Why are they all so big, other children?
So noisy? So much at home they
must have been born in uniform.
Lived all their lives in playgrounds.
Spent the years inventing games
that don't let me in. Games
that are rough, that swallow you up.

And the railings.
All around, the railings.
Are they to keep out wolves and monsters?
Things that carry off and eat children?
Things you don't take sweets from?
Perhaps they're to stop us getting out.
Running away from the lessins. Lessin.
What does a lessin look like?
Sounds small and slimy.
They keep them in glassrooms.
Whole rooms made out of glass. Imagine.

I wish I could remember my name.
Mummy said it would come in useful.
Like wellies. When there's puddles.
Yellowwellies. I wish she was here.
I think my name is sewn on somewhere.
Perhaps the teachers will read it for me.
Tea-cher. The one who makes the tea.

ROGER MCGOUGH

The First Men on Mercury

– We come in peace from the third planet.
Would you take us to your leader?

– Bawr stretter! Bawr. Bawr. Stretterhawl?

– This is a little plastic model
of the solar system, with working parts.
You are here and we are there and we
are now here with you, is this clear?

– Gawl horrop. Bawr. Abawrhannahanna!

– Where we come from is blue and white
with brown, you see we call the brown
here 'land', the blue is 'sea', and the white
is 'clouds' over land and sea, we live
on the surface of the brown land,
all round is sea and clouds. We are 'men'.
Men come –

– Glawp men! Gawrbenner menko. Menhawl?

– Men come in peace from the third planet
which we call 'earth'. We are earthmen.
Take us earthmen to your leader.

　　Thmen? Thmen? Bawr. Bawrhossop.
Yuleeda tan hanna. Harrabost yuleeda.

– I am the yuleeda. You see my hands,
we carry no benner, we come in peace.
The spaceways are all stretterhawn.

– Glawn peacemen all horrabhanna tantko!
Tan come at'mstrossop. Glawp yuleeda!

– Atoms are peacegawl in our harraban.
Menbat worrabost from tan hannahanna.

– You men we know bawrhossoptant. Bawr.
We know yuleeda. Go strawg backspetter quick.

– We cantantabawr, tantingko backspetter now!

– Banghapper now! Yes, third planet back.
Yuleeda will go back blue, white, brown
nowhanna! There is no more talk.

– Gawl han fasthapper?

– No. You must go back to your planet.
Go back in peace, take what you have gained
but quickly.

– Stretterworra gawl, gawl . . .

– Of course, but nothing is ever the same,
now is it? You'll remember Mercury.

EDWIN MORGAN

[164]

The Courts

I always think the Diamond dynasty
A trifle sinister. The King displays
Only one eye: perhaps the other's patched.
The Queen looks unreliable and grasping.
It's true the Knave is one of those who show
Both eyes – but set in a sneering, puffy face.
I'd rather be ruled by Spades, although the King
Seems to rely more on tradition than
His own brains for superiority;
And obviously he married far beneath him.
No doubt the Ace, unique, is the *éminence grise*.
The son, though, looks slick enough to keep the Spades
On top when he succeeds to that great throne.
The Hearts were always beaten by the Spades,
And quite resigned to love and pastries – she,
However, is beginning to look sour.
And then those minor royalties, the Clubs:
Despise them not – their visages are strong.
Their kingdom's poor, remote and mountainous;
But they've been known to work some clever coups.

One thing they share, these flowered families –
Dread of the proletarian Joker, who,
Though warning of his presence by his pallor,
Is always liable to take them by surprise.

ROY FULLER

[165]

Two Riddles

Behold the dual monarchy
Ruling over cutlery.
One's a scald
The other's cold,
But how the tears come pouring down
When you twist that fancy crown.

    *

The more you hold him
The thinner he grows,
The wetter he gets
The brighter he glows,

The lither and leaner
The slimmer his shape,
The more likely he is
To want to escape.

The more he escapes
The more he grows leaner
Each time you touch him
You feel that much cleaner.

    GEORGE SZIRTES

Goose to Donkey

My big friend, I bow help;
I bow Get up, big friend:
let me land-swim again beside your clicky feet,
don't sleep flat with dried wet in your holes.

    LES MURRAY

Hedgehog

The road is slick
in the rain
and good slugs
can be nuzzled
out of shadows
under hedgerows.

I understand.

It's plain
you can't hurry across
even when those other lights
come at you
preceding
the hurtling mountain.

JO SHAPCOTT

The Legend

Some say it was seven tons of meat in a thick black hide
you could build a boat from, stayed close to the river
on the flipside of the sun where the giant forests were.

Had shy, old eyes. You'd need both those hands for one.
Maybe. Walked in placid herds under a jungly, sweating roof
just breathing; a dry electric wind you could hear a mile off.

Huge feet. Some say if it rained you could fish in a footprint,
fruit fell when it passed. It moved, food happened, simple.
You think of a warm, inky cave and you got its mouth all right.

You dream up a yard of sandpaper, damp, you're talking tongue.
Eat? Its own weight in a week. And water. Some say
the sweat steamed from its back in small grey clouds.

But *big*. Enormous. Spine like the mast on a galleon.
Ears like sails gasping for a wind. You picture
a rope you could hang a man from, you're seeing its tail.

Tusks like bannisters. I almost believe myself. Can you
drum up a roar as wide as a continent, a deep hot note
that bellowed out and belonged to the melting air? You got it.

But people have always lied! You know some say it had a trunk
like a soft telescope, that it looked up along it at the sky
and balanced a bright, gone star on the end, and it died.

CAROL ANN DUFFY

Cows

I think
There's a summer ocean liner in cows –
Majestic and far off,
With a quiet mysterious delight
Fading through the blue afternoon.

And there's a ruined holy city
In a herd of lying down, cud-chewing cows –
Noses raised, eyes nearly closed
They are fragments of temples – even their outlines
Still at an angle unearthly.
As if a ray from heaven still rested across their brows,
As if they felt it, a last ray.

And now they come, swinging their ballast, bowing
As if they dragged slow loads slightly uphill,
There's a dance in the swaying walk of cows

With their long dancers' necks, to left and to right
And that slight outfling of hooves, a slow dance step –
Bodies of oil,
Dancers coming from hard labour in the fields.

And there's a flare of wide skirts when they swirl
On such exact feet
With the ankles of tall dancers

In under the girders and asbestos.

TED HUGHES

Bull Song

My bull is white as silvery fish in the river
    white as the egret on the bank
    white as new milk.
His bellowing is as the roar of the Turk's cannon
    from the distant shore.
My bull is dark as raincloud accompanying storm.
He is summer and winter
    half of him dark as thunderhead
    half of him white as sunshine.
His hump shines like the morning star
His forehead is red as the ground hornbill's wattles –
    like a banner,
      seen by the people from afar.

He is like the rainbow.
I shall water him at the river
        and drive my enemies off with my spear.
Let them water their cattle at the well;
        for me and my bull, the river!
Drink, O bull, of the river;
Am I not here with my spear to protect you?

ANONYMOUS
(from the Dinka people of the Sudan, Africa)

Teaching the Parrot

'Say Polly,' whispered Laurie,
But her parrot wouldn't speak.

'Say Polly,' urged Laurie,
And she stroked her parrot's beak,
'Say Polly,'
But her parrot wouldn't speak.

'Say Polly,' begged Laurie,
'Say Polly, will you, please?
Say Polly,' ordered Laurie,
And she got down on her knees.
'Say Polly,' hissed Laurie,
'Come on, just a little squeak,
Say Polly!'
But her parrot wouldn't speak.

'Say Polly,' growled Laurie,
'Just the once and just for me.
Say Polly!' shouted Laurie,
'You're a stupid parrot, see!
Say Polly!' bellowed Laurie,
'Or I'll pluck you for my tea.
Say Polly!!' wailed Laurie,
As the tears rolled down her cheek,
'SAY POLLY!!!' . . .

But her parrot wouldn't speak.

RICHARD EDWARDS

'There was an Old Man with a gong'

There was an Old Man with a gong,
Who bumped at it all the day long;
But they called out, 'O law! you're a horrid old bore!'
So they smashed that Old Man with a gong.

EDWARD LEAR

The Minstrel

I came into the hall
Out of the biting squall:
The snow lay on my shoulders like a shawl.

I heard the monarch call,
Raising his goblet tall,
For a tale to hold the company in thrall –

That told of some great fall
And nicely would appall
Those safely sheltered from the weather's brawl.

I saw fissures in the wall
And things that freely crawl
Over the stones of Egypt, Carthage, Gaul;

And then began to bawl
The tale told by us all,
That starts thuswise: 'I came into the hall . . .'

ROY FULLER

Evidence Read at the Trial of the Knave of Hearts

They told me you had been to her,
    And mentioned me to him:
She gave me a good character,
    But said I could not swim.

He sent them word I had not gone,
    (We know it to be true):
If she should push the matter on,
    What would become of you?

I gave her one, they gave him two,
    You gave us three or more;
They all returned from him to you,
    Though they were mine before.

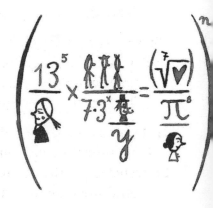

If I or she should chance to be
    Involved in this affair,
He trusts to you to set them free,
    Exactly as we were.

My notion was that you had been
    (Before she had this fit)
An obstacle that came between
    Him, and ourselves, and it.

Don't let him know she liked them best,
    For this must ever be
A secret kept from all the rest,
    Between yourself and me.

LEWIS CARROLL

Jabberwocky

'Twas brillig, and the slithy toves
    Did gyre and gimble in the wabe;
All mimsy were the borogoves,
        And the mome raths outgrabe.

'Beware the Jabberwock, my son!
    The jaws that bite, the claws that catch!
Beware the Jubjub bird, and shun
        The frumious Bandersnatch!'

He took his vorpal sword in hand:
    Long time the manxome foe he sought –
So rested he by the Tumtum tree,
        And stood awhile in thought.

And as in uffish thought he stood,
    The Jabberwock, with eyes of flame,
Came whiffling through the tulgey wood,
        And burbled as it came!

One, two! One, two! And through and through
    The vorpal blade went snicker-snack!
He left it dead, and with its head
      He went galumphing back.

'And hast thou slain the Jabberwock?
    Come to my arms, my beamish boy!
O frabjous day! Callooh! Callay!'
      He chortled in his joy.

'Twas brillig, and the slithy toves
    Did gyre and gimble in the wabe;
All mimsy were the borogoves,
      And the mome raths outgrabe.

LEWIS CARROLL

Korf's Clock

Two pairs of hands go round
on a clock Korf's made
to indicate time advancing,
and time retrograde.

Ten and two it says at once,
it says both three and nine,
and everyone who looks at it
loses his fear of time,

for on this Janus-clock
of Korf's ingenious design
time (as Korf intended)
neutralizes time.

CHRISTIAN MORGENSTERN
(translated by Geoffrey Grigson)

[174]

The Balancing Man

The balancing man
Is a diplomat;
On his cautious head
Sits a balancing hat.

Beneath that hat
I do declare
His brains are measuring
Every hair,

And every hair
Is exactly split
Into what it was
And what was it.

His smile says Now
But his eyes say When.
Never argue
With balancing men.

JOHN MOLE

[175]

Wheelbarrow

He dumped her in the wheelbarrow
   And trundled her away!
How he chaffed and how she laughed
   On their wedding day!

He bumped her through the garden-gate,
   He bounced her down the lane!
Then he reeled and then she squealed,
   And off they bounced again.

He jiggled her across the ditch,
   He joggled her through the holt!
He stubbed his toe and she cried O!
   Whenever she got a jolt.

He wiggled her up the bridle-path,
   He woggled her through the street –
Down he stumbled! down she tumbled,
   Right at the Parson's feet!

ELEANOR FARJEON

Two on a Skateboard

Never mind
that they couldn't go fast.
No bother
that there was none of the usual
rumble-on-concrete whoosh.
They made a beautiful sight,
swanning along with the elegance
of a gondola or punt.

The smaller kid stood behind.
The bigger, up front,
swayed just a touch
on one leg, the other
in its brand-new, brashly white
plaster-cast
angled for balance,
while with a crutch
he gave the occasional, casual
paddle or push.

CHRISTOPHER REID

Song: Lift-Boy

Let me tell you the story of how I began:
I began as the boot-boy and ended as the boot-man,
With nothing in my pockets but a jack-knife and a button,
With nothing in my pockets but a jack-knife and a button,
With nothing in my pockets.

Let me tell you the story of how I went on.
I began as the lift-boy and ended as the lift-man,
With nothing in my pockets but a jack-knife and a button,
With nothing in my pockets but a jack-knife and a button,
With nothing in my pockets.

I found it very easy to whistle and play
With nothing in my head or my pockets all day,
With nothing in my pockets.

But along came Old Eagle, like Moses or David;
He stopped at the fourth floor and preached me Damnation:
'Not a soul shall be savèd, not one shall be savèd.

The whole First Creation shall forfeit salvation:
From knife-boy to lift-boy, from ragged to regal,
Not one shall be savèd, not you, not Old Eagle,
No soul on earth escapeth, even if all repent –'
So I cut the cords of the lift and down we went,
With nothing in our pockets.

ROBERT GRAVES

Nottamun Town

In Nottamun Town not a soul would look up,
Not a soul would look up, not a soul would look down,
Not a soul would look up, not a soul would look down
To tell me the way to Nottamun Town.

I rode a big horse that was called a grey mare,
Grey mane and tail, grey stripes down his back,
Grey mane and tail, grey stripes down his back,
There weren't a hair on him but what was called black.

She stood so still, she threw me to the dirt,
She tore my hide and bruised my shirt;
From stirrup to stirrup I mounted again
And on my ten toes I rode over the plain.

Met the King and the Queen and a company of men
A-walking behind and a-riding before.
A stark naked drummer came walking along
With his hands in his bosom a-beating his drum.

Sat down on a hot and cold frozen stone,
Ten thousand stood round me yet I was alone.

Took my heart in my hand to keep my head warm.
Ten thousand got drowned that never were born.

ANONYMOUS

W

The King sent for his wise men all
     To find a rhyme for W;
When they had thought a good long time
But could not think of a single rhyme,
     'I'm sorry,' said he, 'to trouble you.'

JAMES REEVES

'Go, my son'

'Go, my son, and shut the shutter.'
This I heard a mother utter.
'Shutter's shut,' the boy did mutter.
'I can't shut 'er any shutter.'

JACK PRELUTSKY

Me And Mister Polite

Again and again
we met in the lane.

We met in the sunshine
We met in the rain
We met in the windy

[179]

We met in the hail
We met in the misty
And autumn-leaf trail
On harsh days and dark days
On days mild and clear

And if it was raining
He'd say, 'Nice weather for ducks'
And if it was sunny
He'd say, 'Good enough for beach-wear'
And if it was windy
He'd say, 'We could do without that wind'
And if it was nippy
He'd say, 'Nippy today'
And if it was cold-windy-rainy-grey
(which it nearly always was)
He'd say, 'Horrible day'
Or 'Not as good as it was yesterday'

And he'd hurry away with a brief tip of his hat
His rude dog pulling him this way and that.

GRACE NICHOLS

Pebble

I know a man who's got a pebble.

He found it and he sucked it
during the war.
He found it and he sucked it
when they ran out of water.
He found it and he sucked it
when they were dying for a drink.
And he sucked it and he sucked it
for days and days and days.

I know a man who's got a pebble
and he keeps it in his drawer.

It's small and brown – nothing much to look at
but I think of the things he thinks
when he sees it:
how he found it
how he sucked it
how he nearly died for water to drink.

A small brown pebble
tucked under his tongue
and he keeps it in his drawer
to look at now and then.

MICHAEL ROSEN

Dream Dust

Gather out of star-dust
    Earth-dust,
    Cloud-dust,
    Storm-dust,
And splinters of hail,
One handful of dream-dust
    Not for sale.

LANGSTON HUGHES

Daybreak in Alabama

When I get to be a composer
I'm gonna write me some music about
Daybreak in Alabama
And I'm gonna put the purtiest songs in it
Rising out of the ground like a swamp mist
And falling out of heaven like soft dew.
I'm gonna put some tall tall trees in it
And the scent of pine needles
And the smell of red clay after rain
And long red necks
And poppy colored faces
And big brown arms
And the field daisy eyes
Of black and white black white black people
And I'm gonna put white hands
And black hands and brown and yellow hands
And red clay earth hands in it
Touching everybody with kind fingers

And touching each other natural as dew
In that dawn of music when I
Get to be a composer
And write about daybreak
In Alabama.

LANGSTON HUGHES

Hurricane

Sleep at noon. Window blind
Rattle and bang. Pay no mind.
Door go jump like somebody coming:
let him come. Tin roof drumming:
drum away – she's drummed before.
Blinds blow loose: unlatch the door.
Look up sky through the manchineel:
black show through like a hole in your heel.
Look down shore at the old canoe:
rag-a-tag sea turn white, turn blue,
kick up dust in the lee of the reef,
wallop around like a loblolly leaf.
Let her wallop – who's afraid?
Gale from the north-east: just the Trade . . .

And that's when you hear it: far and high –
sea-birds screaming down the sky
high and far like screaming leaves;
tree-branch slams across the eaves;
rain like pebbles on the ground . . .

and the sea turns white and the wind goes round.

ARCHIBALD MACLEISH

The Hawk

On Sunday the hawk fell on Bigging
    And a chicken screamed
    Lost in its own little snowstorm.
And on Monday he fell on the moor
    And the Field Club
    Raised a hundred silent prisms.
And on Tuesday he fell on the hill
    And the happy lamb
    Never knew why the loud collie straddled him.
And on Wednesday he fell on a bush
    And the blackbird
    Laid by his little flute for the last time.
And on Thursday he fell on Cleat
    And peerie Tom's rabbit
    Swung in a single arc from shore to hill.
And on Friday he fell on a ditch
    But the questing cat,
    That rival, rampant, fluttered his flame.
And on Saturday he fell on Bigging
    And Jock lowered his gun
    And nailed a small wing over the corn.

GEORGE MACKAY BROWN

Five Eyes

In Hans' old Mill his three black cats
Watch his bins for the thieving rats.
Whisker and claw, they crouch in the night,
Their five eyes smouldering green and bright:
Squeaks from the flour sacks, squeaks from where

The cold wind stirs on the empty stair,
Squeaking and scampering, everywhere.
Then down they pounce, now in, now out,
At whisking tail, and sniffing snout;
While lean old Hans he snores away
Till peep of light at break of day;
Then up he climbs to his creaking mill,
Out come his cats all grey with meal –
Jekkel, and Jessup, and one-eyed Jill.

WALTER DE LA MARE

Joker as Told

Not a latch or lock could hold
a little horse we had
not a gate or paddock.

He liked to get in the house.
Walk in, and you were liable
to find him in the kitchen
dribbling over the table
with a heap behind him

or you'd catch a hoof
right where it hurt had
when you went in your bedroom.

He grew up with us kids,
played with us till he got rough.
Round then, they cut him,
but you couldn't ride him:
he'd bite your bum getting on,
kick your foot from the stirrup

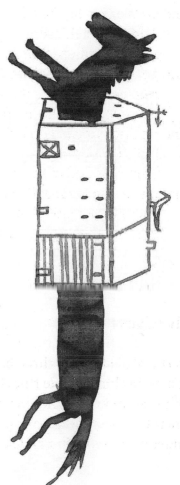

and he could kick the spurs off
your boots. Almost hopped on with you,
and if he couldn't buck you
he'd lie down plop! and roll
in his temper, and he'd squeal.

He was from the Joker breed,
we called him Joker;
no joke much when he bit you
or ate the Monday washing.

They reckon he wanted to be
human, coming in the house.
I don't think so, I think he
wanted something people had.
He didn't do it from love of us.

He couldn't grow up to be a
full horse, and he wouldn't be a slave one.
I think he was looking for his childhood,
his foalhood and ours, when we played.

He was looking for the Kingdom of God.

LES MURRAY

The Runaway

Once when the snow of the year was beginning to fall,
We stopped by a mountain pasture to say, 'Whose colt?'
A little Morgan had one forefoot on the wall,
The other curled at his breast. He dipped his head
And snorted at us. And then he had to bolt.
We heard the miniature thunder where he fled,
And we saw him, or thought we saw him, dim and grey

Like a shadow against the curtain of falling flakes.
'I think the little fellow's afraid of the snow.
He isn't winter-broken. It isn't play
With the little fellow at all. He's running away.
I doubt if even his mother could tell him, "Sakes,
It's only weather." He'd think she didn't know!
Where is his mother? He can't be out alone.'
And now he comes again with clatter of stone,
And mounts the wall again with whited eyes
And all his tail that isn't hair up straight.
He shudders his coat as if to throw off flies.
'Whoever it is that leaves him out so late,
When other creatures have gone to stall and bin,
Ought to be told to come and take him in.'

ROBERT FROST

A Minor Bird

I have wished a bird would fly away,
And not sing by my house all day;

Have clapped my hands at him from the door
When it seemed as if I could bear no more.

The fault must partly have been in me.
The bird was not to blame for his key.

And of course there must be something wrong
In wanting to silence any song.

ROBERT FROST

Burying the Bird

We buried the bird today.

We brought it out on a tray,
Its look was stiff and its feel was chill,
And its eyes were shut and its heart was still.

We buried the bird today.

It was a baby jay,
Its beak was black and its wing was blue,
It was dead as the meat on a barbecue.

We buried the bird today.

Flat on its back it lay,
And both of our cats came sniffing round,
As we found our spot and we dug the ground.

We buried the bird today.

Last night it was quite OK,
And we fed it a worm and we fed it a fly,
And we thought last night that it wouldn't die.

We buried the bird today.

There wasn't a lot to say,
What was warm flesh and blood is just cold skin and bone,
So we scratched its name on a piece of stone.

We buried the bird today.

The sky was all scribbly grey,
Grey as the stone of a pyramid,
And it sat on the world like a dustbin lid.

We buried the bird today.

The shoebox was lined with hay
And flowers and leaves and a pigeon feather,
And we laid the bird in the earth together,

    For ever.

JOHN WHITWORTH

The Bat

The beggarly Bat, a cut-out, scattily
Begs at the lamp's light
A lit moth-mote.

What wraps his shivers?
Scraps of moon cloth
Snatched off cold rivers.

Scissored bits
Of the moon's fashion-crazes
Are his disguises
And wrap up his fits –

For the jittery bat's
Determined to burst
Into day, like the sun

But he never gets past
The dawn's black posts

As long as night lasts
The shuttlecock Bat
Is battered about
By the rackets of ghosts.

TED HUGHES

The New Foal

Yesterday he was nowhere to be found
In the skies or under the skies.

Suddenly he's here – a warm heap
Of ashes and embers, fondled by small draughts.

A star dived from outer space – flared
And burned out in the straw.
Now something is stirring in the smoulder.
We call it a foal.

Still stunned
He has no idea where he is.
His eyes, dew-dusky, explore gloom walls and a glare doorspace.
Is this the world?
It puzzles him. It is a great numbness.

He pulls himself together, getting used to the weight of things
And to that tall horse nudging him, and to this straw.

TED HUGHES

Old Deuteronomy

Old Deuteronomy's lived a long time;
    He's a Cat who has lived many lives in succession.
He was famous in proverb and famous in rhyme
    A long while before Queen Victoria's accession.
Old Deuteronomy's buried nine wives
    And more – I am tempted to say, ninety-nine;
And his numerous progeny prospers and thrives
    And the village is proud of him in his decline.
At the sight of that placid and bland physiognomy,

When he sits in the sun on the vicarage wall,
The Oldest Inhabitant croaks: 'Well, of all . . .
    Things . . . Can it be . . . really! . . . No! . . . Yes! . . .
        Ho! hi!
        Oh, my eye!
My mind may be wandering, but I confess
I *believe* it is Old Deuteronomy!'

Old Deuteronomy sits in the street,
    He sits in the High Street on market day;
The bullocks may bellow, the sheep they may bleat,
    But the dogs and the herdsmen will turn them away.
The cars and the lorries run over the kerb,
    And the villagers put up a notice: ROAD CLOSED –
So that nothing untoward may chance to disturb
    Deuteronomy's rest when he feels so disposed
Or when he's engaged in domestic economy:
    And the Oldest Inhabitant croaks: 'Well, of all . . .
    Things . . . Can it be . . . really! . . . No! . . . Yes! . . .
        Ho! hi!
        Oh, my eye!
My sight's unreliable, but I can guess
That the cause of the trouble is Old Deuteronomy!'

Old Deuteronomy lies on the floor
    Of the Fox and French Horn for his afternoon sleep;
And when the men say: 'There's just time for one more,'
    Then the landlady from her back parlour will peep
And say: 'Now then, out you go, by the back door,
    For Old Deuteronomy mustn't be woken –
I'll have the police if there's any uproar' –
    And out they all shuffle, without a word spoken.
The digestive repose of that feline's gastronomy
    Must never be broken, whatever befall:

And the Oldest Inhabitant croaks: 'Well, of all . . .
   Things . . . Can it be . . . really! . . . Yes! . . . No! . . .
      Ho! hi!
      Oh, my eye!
My legs may be tottery, I must go slow
And be careful of Old Deuteronomy!'

   T. S. ELIOT

'We're all in the dumps'

  We're all in the dumps,
    For diamonds are trumps,
The kittens are gone to Saint Paul's,
    The babies are bit,
    The moon's in a fit,
And the houses are built without walls.

   ANONYMOUS

'I saw Esau'

I saw Esau sawing wood,
And Esau saw I saw him;
Though Esau saw I saw him saw,
Still Esau went on sawing.

   ANONYMOUS

So-So Joe

So-So Joe
de so-so man
wore a so-so suit
with a so-so shoe.
So-So Joe
de so-so man
lived in a so-so house
with a so-so view.
And when you asked
So-so Joe
de so-so man
How do you do?
So-So Joe
de so-so man
would say to you:
      Just so-so
      Nothing new.

JOHN AGARD

Jim Jay

Do diddle di do,
  Poor Jim Jay
Got stuck fast
  In Yesterday.
Squinting he was,
  On cross-legs bent,
Never heeding
  The wind was spent.
Round veered the weathercock,

The sun drew in –
And stuck was Jim
  Like a rusty pin . . .
We pulled and we pulled
  From seven till twelve,
Jim, too frightened
  To help himself.
But all in vain.
  The clock struck one,
And there was Jim
  A little bit gone.
At half-past five
  You scarce could see
A glimpse of his flapping
  Handkerchee.
And when came noon,
  And we climbed sky-high,
Jim was a speck
  Slip – slipping by.
Come to-morrow,
  The neighbours say,
He'll be past crying for:
  Poor Jim Jay.

WALTER DE LA MARE

The Son of the King of Nowhere

When Felix the Tinker came to town
And threw down his shovel money on the counter
Ears went up and eyes looked out
When the Son of the King of Nowhere shouted:

A large Black Bush and a pint of Guinness
And one of your meat and potato pies, missis
And have a drink yourself. That's grand. Cheers!
Here's health! 'Slainte and farewell to care!'
Is the call of the Son of the King of Nowhere.

And the music started and Felix danced
His lunging, lurking, staggering dance,
Stopping wall-eyed and sweating,
Face burning, staring into the air.
So who wants to fight? I'll part his hair!
He'll be sorry he met the Son of the King of Nowhere.

But oh, Felix, when the lights were out in the snug
And the dog sleeping on the rug
And the porter rings drying on the unwiped copper,
You crawled away to your Winter Palace, that cold corner
In Rat Street and huddled up your tinker's
Dreams with the cold old moon rolling
On the rooftops.

And then you gave a curse for the world,
Coiled up like an old moggy cat in that bare
Room, lost and lonely, just you only,
Tinker prince, Son of the King of Nowhere.

    MIKE HARDING

Seumas Beg

A man was sitting underneath a tree
Outside the village; and he asked me what
Name was upon this place; and said that he
Was never here before – He told a lot

Of stories to me too. His nose was flat!
I asked him how it happened, and he said
– The first mate of the *Mary Anne* did that
With a marling-spike one day – but he was dead,

And jolly good job too; and he'd have gone
A long way to have killed him – Oh, he had
A gold ring in one ear; the other one
– 'Was bit off by a crocodile, bedad!'

That's what he said. He taught me how to chew!
He was a real nice man. He liked me too!

JAMES STEPHENS

Who's In?

'The door is shut fast
    And everyone's out.'
But people don't know
    What they're talking about!
Say the fly on the wall,
And the flame on the coals,
And the dog on his rug,
And the mice in their holes,
And the kitten curled up,
And the spiders that spin –
'What, everyone out?
Why, everyone's in!'

ELIZABETH FLEMING

Mushrooms

Overnight, very
Whitely, discreetly,
Very quietly

Our toes, our noses
Take hold on the loam,
Acquire the air.

Nobody sees us,
Stops us, betrays us;
The small grains make room.

Soft fists insist on
Heaving the needles,
The leafy bedding,

Even the paving.
Our hammers, our rams,
Earless and eyeless,

Perfectly voiceless,
Widen the crannies,
Shoulder through holes. We

Diet on water,
On crumbs of shadow,
Bland mannered, asking

Little or nothing.
So many of us!
So many of us!

We are shelves, we are
Tables, we are meek,
We are edible,

Nudgers and shovers
In spite of ourselves.
Our kind multiplies:

We shall by morning
Inherit the earth.
Our foot's in the door.

SYLVIA PLATH

Snail

With skin all wrinkled
Like a Whale
On a ribbon of sea
Comes the moonlit Snail.

The Cabbage murmurs:
'I feel something's wrong!'
The Snail says 'Shhh!
I am God's tongue.'

The Rose shrieks out:
'What's this? O what's this?'
The Snail says: 'Shhh!
I am God's kiss.'

So the whole garden
(Till stars fail)
Suffers the passion
Of the Snail.

TED HUGHES

Take-over by the Garden

In the end, the garden creatures became more friendly.
The ladybird led by refusing to fly from our finger –
More than usually – fluffing her wings out from their cases
Then putting them very neatly back again.

The blackbird didn't stop at the threshold, but showed
The bald rings round his eyes, his earth-crumbed bill,
His white chinks in his glossy armour of black,
Among the curving chair-legs and our slippers.

And the dusty bristles of the hedgehog made
Our sofas difficult to lie on: bees
Drank with us at our bedside tumblers of water:
In the bath, living frogs as well as plastic dolphins.

And no one seemed to quarrel in front of the owl,
Standing at the end of the shelf like a loudspeaker.
Our lives were full of little important cares;
And happily this happened all the world over.

ROY FULLER

Mole

I am the Mole.
Not easy to know.
Wherever I go
I travel by hole.

My hill-making hand
Is the best of me.
As a seal under sea
I swim under land.

My nose hunts bright
As a beam of light.
With the prick of a pin
My eyes were put in.

Your telly's there.
You feast as you stare.
Worms are my diet.
In dark and in quiet

I don't eat alone.
At my table sit
Centurion
And Ancient Brit.

TED HUGHES

Too Many Daves

Did I ever tell you that Mrs McCave
Had twenty-three sons and she named them all Dave?
Well, she did. And that wasn't a smart thing to do.
You see, when she wants one and calls out, 'Yoo-Hoo!
Come into the house, Dave!' she doesn't get one.
All twenty-three Daves of hers come on the run!
This makes things quite difficult at the McCaves'
As you can imagine, with so many Daves.
And often she wishes that, when they were born,
She had named one of them Bodkin Van Horn
And one of them Hoos-Foos. And one of them Snimm.
And one of them Hot-Shot. And one Sunny Jim.
And one of them Shadrack. And one of them Blinkey.
And one of them Stuffy. And one of them Stinkey.
Another one Putt-Putt. Another one Moon Face.

Another one Marvin O'Gravel Balloon Face.
And one of them Ziggy. And one Soggy Muff.
One Buffalo Bill. And one Biffalo Buff.
And one of them Sneepy. And one Weepy Weed.
And one Paris Garters. And one Harris Tweed.
And one of them Sir Michael Carmichael Zutt
And one of them Oliver Boliver Butt
And one of them Zanzibar Buck-Buck McFate . . .
But she didn't do it. And now it's too late.

DR SEUSS (THEODORE GEISEL)

Something to Worry About

Nothing rhymes wid **nothing**
I discovered dat today
Now I hav two more words
To help me rhyme away,
Nothing + **nothing** = **nothing**
I am good at maths as well
I feel like a professor
As me head begins to swell.

If I start wid **nothing**
I hav **nothing** to lose
And now dat I hav two **nothings**
It's easier to choose,
Nothing gets me worried
I hope you overstand
I am now enjoying **nothing**
And I hav **nothing** planned.

I am busy doing **nothing**
Me parents think it's great
I am in luv wid **nothing**
And there's **nothing** dat I hate,
I will give you **nothing**
So you hav **nothing** to fear
Let me tell you **nothing**
I hav **nothing** to declare.

Nothing's rong wid **nothing**
It's such a great idea
It need not be created
I hav **nothing** to share,
Nothing rhymes wid **nothing**
There waz **nothing** at de start
And I can't give you anything
When there's **nothing** in my heart.

BENJAMIN ZEPHENIAH

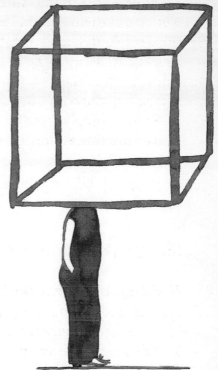

The Sound Collector

A stranger called this morning
Dressed all in black and grey
Put every sound into a bag
And carried them away

The whistling of the kettle
The turning of the lock
The purring of the kitten
The ticking of the clock

The popping of the toaster
The crunching of the flakes

When you spread the marmalade
The scraping noise it makes

The hissing of the frying-pan
The ticking of the grill
The bubbling of the bathtub
As it starts to fill

The drumming of the raindrops
On the window-pane
When you do the washing-up
The gurgle of the drain

The crying of the baby
The squeaking of the chair
The swishing of the curtain
The creaking of the stair

A stranger called this morning
He didn't leave his name
Left us only silence
Life will never be the same.

ROGER MCGOUGH

The Pied Piper of Hamelin

I

Hamelin Town's in Brunswick,
    By famous Hanover city;
The river Weser, deep and wide,
Washes its wall on the southern side;
A pleasanter spot you never spied;
    But, when begins my ditty,

Almost five hundred years ago,
To see the townsfolk suffer so
    From vermin, was a pity.

II

    Rats!
They fought the dogs and killed the cats,
    And bit the babies in the cradles,
And ate the cheeses out of the vats,
    And licked the soup from the cooks' own ladles,
Split open the kegs of salted sprats,
Made nests inside men's Sunday hats,
And even spoiled the women's chats
        By drowning their speaking
        With shrieking and squeaking
In fifty different sharps and flats.

III

At last the people in a body
    To the Town Hall came flocking:
''Tis clear,' cried they, 'our Mayor's a noddy;
    And as for our Corporation – shocking
To think we buy gowns lined with ermine
For dolts that can't or won't determine
What's best to rid us of our vermin!
You hope, because you're old and obese,
To find in the furry civic robe ease?
Rouse up, sirs! Give your brains a racking
To find the remedy we're lacking,
Or, sure as fate, we'll send you packing!'
At this the Mayor and Corporation
Quaked with a mighty consternation.

IV

An hour they sat in council,
    At length the Mayor broke silence:
'For a guilder I'd my ermine gown sell,
    I wish I were a mile hence!
It's easy to bid one rack one's brain –
I'm sure my poor head aches again,
I've scratched it so, and all in vain.
Oh, for a trap, a trap, a trap!'
Just as he said this, what should hap
At the chamber door but a gentle tap?
'Bless us,' cried the Mayor, 'what's that?'
(With the Corporation as he sat,
Looking little though wondrous fat;
Nor brighter was his eye, nor moister
Than a too-long-opened oyster,
Save when at noon his paunch grew mutinous
For a plate of turtle, green and glutinous)
'Only a scraping of shoes on the mat?
Anything like the sound of a rat
Makes my heart go pit-a-pat!'

V

'Come in!' the Mayor cried, looking bigger:
And in did come the strangest figure!
His queer long coat from heel to head
Was half of yellow and half of red,
And he himself was tall and thin,
With sharp blue eyes, each like a pin,
And light loose hair, yet swarthy skin,
No tuft on cheek nor beard on chin,
But lips where smiles went out and in;

There was no guessing his kith and kin:
And nobody could enough admire
The tall man and his quaint attire.
Quoth one: 'It's as my great-grandsire,
Starting up at the Trump of Doom's tone,
Had walked this way from his painted tombstone!'

VI

He advanced to the council-table:
And, 'Please your honours,' said he, 'I'm able,
By means of a secret charm, to draw
    All creatures living beneath the sun,
    That creep or swim or fly or run,
After me so as you never saw!
And I chiefly use my charm
On creatures that do people harm,
The mole and toad and newt and viper;
And people call me the Pied Piper.'
(And here they noticed round his neck
    A scarf of red and yellow stripe,
To match with his coat of the self-same check;
    And at the scarf's end hung a pipe;
And his fingers, they noticed, were ever straying
As if impatient to be playing
Upon this pipe, as low it dangled
Over his vesture so old-fangled.)
'Yet,' said he, 'poor piper as I am,
In Tartary I freed the Cham,
    Last June, from his huge swarms of gnats;
I eased in Asia the Nizam
    Of a monstrous brood of vampire-bats:
And as for what your brain bewilders,
    If I can rid your town of rats

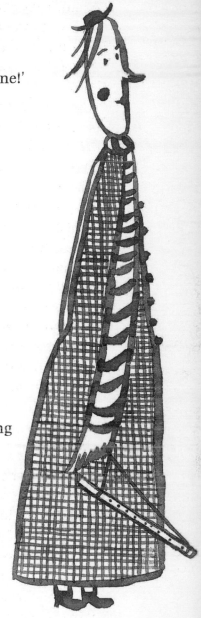

Will you give me a thousand guilders?'
'One? fifty thousand!' – was the exclamation
Of the astonished Mayor and Corporation.

VII

Into the street the Piper stept,
   Smiling first a little smile,
As if he knew what magic slept
   In his quiet pipe the while;
Then, like a musical adept,
To blow the pipe his lips he wrinkled,
And green and blue his sharp eyes twinkled,
Like a candle-flame where salt is sprinkled;
And ere three shrill notes the pipe uttered,
You heard as if an army muttered;
And the muttering grew to a grumbling;
And the grumbling grew to a mighty rumbling;
And out of the houses the rats came tumbling,
Great rats, small rats, lean rats, brawny rats,
Brown rats, black rats, grey rats, tawny rats,
Grave old plodders, gay young friskers,
   Fathers, mothers, uncles, cousins,
Cocking tails and pricking whiskers,
   Families by tens and dozens,
Brothers, sisters, husbands, wives –
Followed the Piper for their lives.
From street to street he piped advancing,
And step for step they followed dancing,
Until they came to the river Weser,
   Wherein all plunged and perished!
– Save one who, stout as Julius Caesar,
Swam across and lived to carry
   (As he, the manuscript he cherished)

To Rat-land home his commentary:
Which was, 'At the first shrill notes of the pipe,
I heard a sound as of scraping tripe,
And putting apples, wondrous ripe,
Into a cider-press's gripe:
And a moving away of pickle-tub-boards,
And a leaving ajar of conserve-cupboards,
And a drawing the corks of train-oil-flasks,
And a breaking the hoops of butter-casks;
And it seemed as if a voice
    (Sweeter far than by harp or by psaltery
Is breathed) called out, "Oh rats, rejoice!
    The world is grown to one vast drysaltery!
So munch on, crunch on, take your nuncheon,
Breakfast, supper, dinner, luncheon!"
And just as a bulky sugar-puncheon,
All ready staved, like a great sun shone
Glorious scarce an inch before me,
Just as methought it said, "Come, bore me!"
– I found the Weser rolling o'er me.'

    VIII

You should have heard the Hamelin people
Ringing the bells till they rocked the steeple.
'Go,' cried the Mayor 'and get long poles,
Poke out the nests and block up the holes!
Consult with carpenters and builders,
And leave in our town not even a trace
Of the rats!' – when suddenly, up the face
Of the Piper perked in the market-place,
With a 'First, if you please, my thousand guilders!'

IX

A thousand guilders! The Mayor looked blue;
So did the Corporation too.
For council dinners made rare havoc
With Claret, Moselle, Vin-de-Grave, Hock;
And half the money would replenish
Their cellar's biggest butt with Rhenish.
To pay this sum to a wandering fellow
With a gipsy coat of red and yellow!
'Beside,' quoth the Mayor with a knowing wink,
'Our business was done at the river's brink;
We saw with our eyes the vermin sink,
And what's dead can't come to life, I think.
So, friend, we're not the folks to shrink
From the duty of giving you something for drink,
And a matter of money to put in your poke;
But as for the guilders, what we spoke
Of them, as you very well know, was in joke.
Besides, our losses have made us thrifty.
A thousand gilders! Come, take fifty!'

X

The Piper's face fell, and he cried
'No trifling! I can't wait, beside!
I've promised to visit by dinnertime
Baghdad, and accept the prime
Of the Head-Cook's pottage, all he's rich in,
For having left, in the Caliph's kitchen,
Of a nest of scorpions no survivor:
With him I proved no bargain-driver,
With you, don't think I'll bate a stiver!
And folks who put me in a passion
May find me pipe after another fashion.'

XI

'How?' cried the Mayor, 'd'ye think I brook
Being worse treated than a cook?
Insulted by a lazy ribald
With idle pipe and vesture piebald?
You threaten us, fellow? Do your worst,
Blow your pipe there till you burst!'

XII

Once more he stepped into the street
    And to his lips again
    Laid his long pipe of smooth straight cane;
And ere he blew three notes (such sweet
Soft notes as yet musician's cunning
    Never gave the enraptured air)
There was a rustling that seemed like a bustling
Of merry crowds justling at pitching and hustling
Small feet were pattering, wooden shoes clattering,
Little hands clapping and little tongues chattering,
And, like fowls in a farmyard when barley is scattering,
Out came the children running.
All the little boys and girls,
With rosy cheeks and flaxen curls,
And sparkling eyes and teeth like pearls,
Tripping and skipping, ran merrily after
The wonderful music with shouting and laughter.

XIII

The Mayor was dumb, and the Council stood
As if they were changed into blocks of wood,
Unable to move a step, or cry
To the children merrily skipping by

– Could only follow with the eye
That joyous crowd at the Piper's back.
But how the Mayor was on the rack,
And the wretched Council's bosoms beat,
As the Piper turned from the High Street
To where the Weser rolled its waters
Right in the way of their sons and daughters!
However he turned from south to west,
And to Koppelberg Hill his steps addressed,
And after him the children pressed;
Great was the joy in every breast.
'He never can cross that mighty top!
He's forced to let the piping drop,
And we shall see our children stop!'
When, lo, as they reached the mountain-side,
A wondrous portal opened wide,
As if a cavern was suddenly hollowed;
And the Piper advanced and the children followed,
And when all were in to the very last,
The door in the mountain-side shut fast.
Did I say, all? No! One was lame,
    And could not dance the whole of the way;
And in after years, if you would blame
    His sadness, he was used to say –
'It's dull in our town since my playmates left!
I can't forget that I'm bereft
Of all the pleasant sights they see,
Which the Piper also promised me.
For he led us, he said, to a joyous land,
Joining the town and just at hand,
Where waters gushed and fruit trees grew
And flowers put forth a fairer hue,
And everything was strange and new;

The sparrows were brighter than peacocks here,
And their dogs outran our fallow deer,
And honey-bees had lost their stings,
And horses were born with eagles' wings:
And just as I became assured
My lame foot would be speedily cured,
The music stopped and I stood still,
And found myself outside the hill,
Left alone against my will,
To go now limping as before,
And never hear of that country more!'

XIV

Alas, alas for Hamelin!
    There came into many a burgher's pate
    A text which says that heaven's gate
    Opes to the rich at as easy rate
As the needle's eye takes a camel in!
The Mayor sent east, west, north, and south,
To offer the Piper, by word of mouth,
    Wherever it was men's lot to find him,
Silver and gold to his heart's content,
If he'd only return the way he went,
    And bring the children behind him.
But when they saw 'twas a lost endeavour,
And Piper and dancers were gone for ever,
They made a decree that lawyers never
    Should think their records dated duly
If, after the day of the month and year,
These words did not as well appear,
'And so long after what happened here
    On the Twenty-second of July,

Thirteen hundred and seventy-six':
And the better in memory to fix
The place of the children's last retreat,
They called it the Pied Piper's Street –
Where anyone playing on pipe or tabor
Was sure for the future to lose his labour.
Nor suffered they hostelry or tavern
    To shock with mirth a street so solemn;
But opposite the place of the cavern
    They wrote the story on a column;
And on the great church-window painted
The same, to make the world acquainted
How their children were stolen away,
And there it stands to this very day.
And I must not omit to say
That in Transylvania there's a tribe
Of alien people who ascribe
The outlandish ways and dress
On which their neighbours lay such stress,
To their fathers and mothers having risen
Out of some subterraneous prison
Into which they were trepanned
Long time ago in a mighty band
Out of Hamelin town in Brunswick land,
But how or why, they don't understand.

    XV

So, Willy, let you and me be wipers
Of scores out with all men – especially pipers!
And, whether they pipe us free from rats or from mice,
If we've promised them aught, let us keep our promise!

ROBERT BROWNING

[214]

'He was a rat'

He was a rat, and she was a rat,
    And down in one hole they did dwell,
And both were as black as a witch's cat,
    And they loved one another well.

He had a tail, and she had a tail,
    Both long and curling and fine;
And each said, 'Yours is the finest tail
    In the world, excepting mine.'

He smelt the cheese, and she smelt the cheese,
    And they both pronounced it good;
And both remarked it would greatly add
    To the charms of their daily food.

So he ventured out, and she ventured out,
    And I saw them go with pain,
But what befell them I never can tell,
    For they never came back again.

ANONYMOUS

Tom Bone

My name is Tom Bone,
I live all alone
In a deep house on Winter Street.
    Through my mud wall
    The wolf-spiders crawl
    And the mole has his beat.

On my roof of green grass
All the day footsteps pass
In the heat and the cold,
    As snug in a bed
    With my name at its head
    One great secret I hold.

Tom Bone, when the owls rise
In the drifting night skies
Do you walk round about?
    All the solemn hours through
    I lie down just like you
    And sleep the night out.

Tom Bone, as you lie there
On your pillow of hair,
What grave thoughts do you keep?
    Tom says, Nonsense and stuff!
    You'll know soon enough.
    Sleep, darling, sleep.

CHARLES CAUSLEY

Hallowe'en

It is Hallowe'en. Turnip Head
Will soon be given his face,
A slit, two triangles, a hole.
His brains litter the table top.
A candle stub will be his soul.

MICHAEL LONGLEY

The Babes in the Wood

My dear, do you know
How a long time ago,
  Two poor little children,
Whose names I don't know,
Were stolen away
On a fine summer's day,
  And left in a wood,
As I've heard people say.

And when it was night,
So sad was their plight,
  The sun it went down,
And the moon gave no light!
They sobbed and they sighed,
And they bitterly cried,
  And the poor little things,
They lay down and died.

And when they were dead,
The robins so red
  Brought strawberry leaves
And over them spread;
And all the day long,
They sang them this song –
  Poor babes in the wood!
  Poor babes in the wood!
And won't you remember
  The babes in the wood?

ANONYMOUS

[217]

A Dirge

Call for the robin red-breast and the wren,
Since o'er shady groves they hover,
And with leaves and flowers do cover
The friendless bodies of unburied men.
Call unto his funeral dole
The ant, the field-mouse, and the mole,
To rear him hillocks that shall keep him warm,
And (when gay tombs are robbed) sustain no harm;
But keep the wolf far thence, that's foe to men,
For with his nails he'll dig them up again.

JOHN WEBSTER

Please to Remember

Here am I,
A poor old Guy:
Legs in a bonfire,
Head in the sky;

Shoeless my toes,
Wild stars behind,
Smoke in my nose,
And my eye-peeps blind;

Old hat, old straw –
In this disgrace;
While the wildfire gleams
On a mask for face.

Ay, all I am made of
Only trash is;

And soon – soon,
Will be dust and ashes.

WALTER DE LA MARE

The Lonely Scarecrow

My poor old bones – I've only two –
A broomshank and a broken stave,
My ragged gloves are a disgrace,
My one peg-foot is in the grave.

I wear the labourer's old clothes;
Coat, shirt and trousers all undone.
I bear my cross upon a hill
In rain and shine, in snow and sun.

I cannot help the way I look.
My funny hat is full of hay.
– O, wild birds, come and nest in me!
Why do you always fly away?

JAMES KIRKUP

'Hopping frog'

Hopping frog, hop here and be seen,
    I'll not pelt you with stick or stone:
Your cap is laced and your coat is green;
    Goodbye, we'll let each other alone.

CHRISTINA ROSSETTI

The Snare

I hear a sudden cry of pain!
   There is a rabbit in a snare:
Now I hear the cry again,
   But I cannot tell from where.

But I cannot tell from where
   He is calling out for aid;
Crying on the frightened air,
   Making everything afraid,

Making everything afraid
   Wrinkling up his little face,
As he cries again for aid;
   – And I cannot find the place!

And I cannot find the place
   Where his paw is in the snare;
Little one! Oh, little one!
   I am searching everywhere!

JAMES STEPHENS

Memoirs of a Fallen Blackbird

They liked me when I was on the wing
And I could whistle and I could sing;
But now that I am in my bed of clay
They come no more for to be with me.

It was on the main road half-way between
Newcastle West and Abbeyfeale;

A juggernaut glanced me as it passed me by
And that was the end of the road for me.

Later that day, as I lay on the verge,
A thin rake of a young man picked me up
Into his trembling hands, and he stared
At me full quarter of an hour, he stared

At me and then he laid me down
And with his hands scooped me a shallow grave;
His soul passed into me as he covered me o'er;
I fear for him now where'er he be.

They liked me when I was on the wing
And I could whistle and I could sing;
But now that I am in my bed of clay
They come no more for to be with me.

    PAUL DURCAN

'There's been a Death'

There's been a Death, in the Opposite House,
As lately as Today –
I know it, by the numb look
Such Houses have – alway –

The Neighbors rustle in and out –
The Doctor – drives away –
A Window opens like a Pod –
Abrupt – mechanically –

Somebody flings a Mattress out –
The Children hurry by –

They wonder if it died – on that –
I used to – when a Boy –

The Minister – goes stiffly in –
As if the House were His –
And He owned all the Mourners – now –
And little Boys – besides –

And then the Milliner – and the Man
Of the Appalling Trade –
To take the measure of the House –

There'll be that Dark Parade –

Of Tassels – and of Coaches – soon –
It's easy as a Sign –
The Intuition of the News –
In Just a Country Town –

EMILY DICKINSON

'Bee! I'm expecting you!'

Bee! I'm expecting you!
Was saying Yesterday
To Somebody you know
That you were due –

The Frogs got Home last Week –
Are settled, and at work –
Birds, mostly back –
The Clover warm and thick –

You'll get my Letter by
The seventeenth; Reply

Or better, be with me –
Yours, Fly.

EMILY DICKINSON

Winter Trees

Aren't you cold and won't you freeze,
With branches bare, you winter trees?
You've thrown away your summer shift,
Your autumn gold has come adrift.

Dearie me, you winter trees,
What strange behaviour if you please!
In summer, you could wear much less,
But come the winter, you undress!

ZOLTÁN ZELK
(*translated by George Szirtes*)

Disillusionment of Ten O'Clock

The houses are haunted
By white night-gowns.
None are green,
Or purple with green rings,
Or green with yellow rings,
Or yellow with blue rings.
None of them are strange,
With socks of lace
And beaded ceintures.
People are not going
To dream of baboons and periwinkles.

Only, here and there, an old sailor,
Drunk and asleep in his boots,
Catches tigers
In red weather.

WALLACE STEVENS

Dinky

O what's the weather in a Beard?
It's windy there, and rather weird,
And when you think the sky has cleared
   – Why, there is Dirty Dinky.

Suppose you walk out in a Storm
With nothing on to keep you warm,
And then step barefoot on a Worm
   – Of course, it's Dirty Dinky.

As I was crossing a hot hot Plain,
I saw a sight that caused me pain,
You asked me before, I'll tell you again:
   – It *looked* like Dirty Dinky.

Last night you lay a-sleeping? No!
The room was thirty-five below;
The sheets and blankets turned to snow.
   – He'd got in: Dirty Dinky.

You'd better watch the things you do.
You'd better watch the things you do.
You're part of him; he's part of you
   – *You* may be Dirty Dinky.

THEODORE ROETHKE

'The night was growing old'

The night was growing old
   As she trudged through snow and sleet;
And her nose was long and cold,
   And her shoes were full of feet.

ANONYMOUS

Meg Merrilies

Old Meg she was a Gipsy
   And liv'd upon the Moors:
Her bed it was the brown heath turf,
   And her house was out of doors.

Her apples were swart blackberries,
   Her currants pods o' broom;
Her wine was dew o' the wild white rose
   Her book a churchyard tomb.

Her Brothers were the craggy hills,
   Her Sisters larchen trees –
Alone with her great family
   She liv'd as she did please.

No breakfast had she many a morn,
   No dinner many a noon,
And 'stead of supper she would stare
   Full hard against the Moon.

But every morn of woodbine fresh
   She made her garlanding,

And every night the dark glen Yew
    She wove, and she would sing.

And with her fingers old and brown
    She plaited Mats o' Rushes,
And gave them to the Cottagers
    She met among the Bushes.

Od Meg was brave as Margaret Queen
    And tall as Amazon:
An old red blanket cloak she wore;
    A chip hat had she on.
God rest her aged bones somewhere –
    She died full long agone!

JOHN KEATS

What I Did in Town

I said:
I'll tell you what I did in town
I saw a greengrocer in the underground
with his pockets full of oranges,
a paperboy yawned
so you could see his tonsils,
there was one old football boot
lying in city square
and round the island came the Odeon commissionaire
riding on a moped with his uniform flying,
a hamster saw a parrot sneeze
the shop blinds flapped and an oiltanker squealed,
the peanut man
lost a bag beneath a bus's wheels

'Mind your peanuts' a girl shouted
his tray was slipping and a taxi hooted
'O help me then' he called out
I said: 'where I'm sorry where'
and forty thousand pigeons climbed into the air.

MICHAEL ROSEN

Buying Your Voice

I want to buy your voice.
There is a kiosk
down the street
where it is sold.
I've been saving up
for a while to have it.
You will hear me paying for it
in California, Kate,
and we will blab
to the value of ten pounds.
When the last coin has been used
the machine will bleep
and no matter how loudly we scream
no sound will come through.

JULIE O'CALLAGHAN

Ten Pence Story

Out of the melting pot, into the mint;
next news I was loose change for a Leeds pimp,

burning a hole in his skin-tight pocket
till he tipped a busker by the precinct.

Not the most ceremonious release
for a fresh faced coin still cutting its teeth.
But that's my point: if you're poorly bartered
you're scuppered before you've even started.

My lowest ebb was a seven month spell
spent head down in a stagnant wishing well,
half eclipsed by an oxidized tuppence
which impressed me with its green circumference.

When they fished me out I made a few phone calls,
fed a few meters, hung round the pool halls.
I slotted in well, but all that vending
blunted my edges and did my head in.

Once, I came within an ace of the end
on the stern of a North Sea ferry, when
some half-cut, ham-fisted cockney tossed me
up into the air and almost dropped me

and every transaction flashed before me
like a time lapse autobiography.
Now, just the thought of travel by water
lifts the serrations around my border.

Some day I know I'll be bagged up and sent
to that knacker's yard for the over spent
to be broken, boiled, unmade and replaced,
for my metals to go their separate ways . . .

which is sad. All coins have dreams. Some castings
from my own batch, I recall, were hatching

an exchange scam on the foreign market
and some inside jobs on one arm bandits.

My own ambition? Well, that was simple:
to be flipped in Wembley's centre circle,
to twist, to turn, to hang like a planet,
to touch down on that emerald carpet.

Those with faith in the system say 'don't quit,
bide your time, if you're worth it, you'll make it.'
But I was robbed, I was badly tendered.
I could have scored. I could have contended.

SIMON ARMITAGE

'I Saw'

I saw a peacock with a fiery tail
I saw a blazing comet drop down hail
I saw a cloud with ivy circled round
I saw a sturdy oak creep on the ground
I saw an ant swallow up a whale
I saw a raging sea brim full of ale
I saw a Venice glass sixteen foot deep
I saw a well full of men's tears that weep
I saw their eyes all in a flame of fire
I saw a house as big as the moon and higher
I saw the sun even in the midst of night
I saw the man that saw this wondrous sight.

I saw a fishpond all on fire
I saw a house bow to a squire
I saw a parson twelve feet high
I saw a cottage near the sky

I saw a balloon made of lead
I saw a coffin drop down dead
I saw a sparrow run a race
I saw two horses making lace
I saw a girl just like a cat
I saw a kitten wear a hat
I saw a man who saw these too,
And says, though strange, they all are true.

ANONYMOUS

The Crystal Cabinet

The Maiden caught me in the Wild,
Where I was dancing merrily;
She put me into her Cabinet
And Lock'd me up with a golden Key.

This Cabinet is form'd of Gold
And Pearl & Crystal shining bright,
And within it opens into a World
And a little lovely Moony Night.

Another England there I saw,
Another London with its Tower,
Another Thames & other Hills,
And another pleasant Surrey Bower,

Another Maiden like herself,
Translucent, lovely, shining clear,
Threefold each in the other clos'd –
O, what a pleasant trembling fear!

O, what a smile! a threefold Smile
Fill'd me, that like a flame I burn'd;
I bent to Kiss the lovely Maid,
And found a Threefold Kiss return'd.

I strove to seize the inmost Form
With ardor fierce & hands of flame,
But burst the Crystal Cabinet,
And like a Weeping Babe became –

A weeping Babe upon the wild,
And Weeping Woman pale reclin'd,
And in the outward air again
I fill'd with woes the passing Wind.

WILLIAM BLAKE

Our Bog is Dood

Our Bog is dood, our Bog is dood,
They lisped in accents mild,
But when I asked them to explain
They grew a little wild.
How do you know your Bog is dood
My darling little child?

We know because we wish it so
That is enough, they cried,
And straight within each infant eye
Stood up the flame of pride,
And if you do not think it so
You shall be crucified.

Then tell me, darling little ones,
What's dood, suppose Bog is?
Just what we think, the answer came,
Just what we think it is.
They bowed their heads. Our Bog is ours
And we are wholly his.

But when they raised them up again
They had forgotten me
Each one upon each other glared
In pride and misery
For what was dood, and what their Bog
They never could agree.

Oh sweet it was to leave them then,
And sweeter not to see,
And sweetest of all to walk alone
Beside the encroaching sea,
The sea that soon should drown them all,
That never yet drowned me.

STEVIE SMITH

Ariel's Song

Full fathom five thy father lies;
   Of his bones are coral made;
Those are pearls that were his eyes:
   Nothing of him that doth fade,
But doth suffer a sea-change
Into something rich and strange:
Sea-nymphs hourly ring his knell.
   Ding-dong!
Hark! now I hear them,
– Ding-dong, bell!

WILLIAM SHAKESPEARE

Night School

Somehow I'm back, at the back of the class
behind the same old heads and shoulders.
   But it's dark.

Only a slantwise rod of moonlight on the floor
at the feet of the figure in black who creaks
   chalk on the board.

And whatever it was we were meant to be learning
I can't for the life of me think. So long ago . . .
   Now he turns

and just as I'm going to have to see his face
he sinks with his head in his hands. His script
   is faint as spider's lace:

I cannot teach you any more.

In front of each of us, a sealed envelope . . .
Our end-of-term reports. It's so hard to resist.
    'Do not open

on pain of . . .' Billy next to me, he's eased
his open. He slips the paper out. He squints.
    he drops it. *Please,*

Sir – his voice is an old man's whisper – *May I
be excused?* The paper lies there: 'William
    Hope. Passed away

May 13th, 2036, aged 55. RIP.'
It's a clip from *The Times*. So we know
    what the teacher means

as he looks up with his hollow eyes, his sunken jaw:

I cannot teach you any more.

PHILIP GROSS

History Lesson

    First, one
in the crowd puts the eye on you –
a nod to number two

    who gets the message
and flips back something side-
long, something snide

    that everybody hears
but you. Soon three or four
are in it. They'll make sure

you catch the steel
glint of the snigger they wear
like a badge. And there

   come five or six
together, casual, shouldering in
around you with a single grin

   and nothing you say
seems to reach them at all.
The badmouthings they call

   mean only this:
they want to scratch. You are the itch.
A thousand years stand by, hissing *Witch!*

   Nigger! Yid!
All you hear is silence lumbered
shut around you. And the ten or hundred

   looking on
look on. They are learning not to see.
The bell rings, too late. Already

   this is history.

PHILIP GROSS

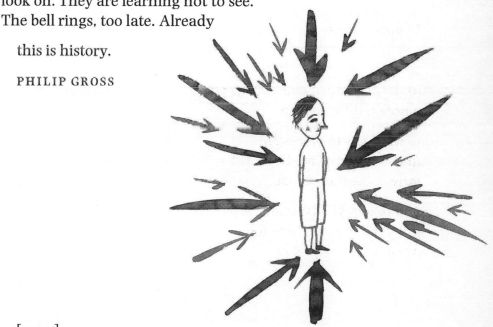

Stevie Scared

Stevie Scared, scared of the dark,
Scared of rats, of dogs that bark,
Scared of his fat dad, scared of his mother,
Scared of his sis and his tattooed brother,
Scared of tall girls, scared of boys,
Scared of ghosts and sudden noise,
Scared of spiders, scared of bees,
Scared of standing under trees,
Scared of shadows, scared of adders,
Scared of the devil, scared of ladders,
Scared of hailstones, scared of rain,
Scared of falling down the drain,
Stevie Scared, scared of showing
He's so scared and people knowing,
Spends his whole time kicking, fighting,
Shoving, pinching, butting, biting,
Bashing little kids about
(Just in case they find him out).

RICHARD EDWARDS

Dear Mum,

while you were out
a cup went and broke itself,
a crack appeared in the blue vase
your great-great grandad
brought back from China.
Somehow, without me even turning on the tap,
the sink mysteriously overflowed.

A strange jam-stain
about the size of a boy's hand,
appeared on the kitchen wall.
I don't think we will ever discover
exactly how the cat
managed to turn on the washing-machine
(specially from the inside),
or how the self-raising flour
managed to self raise.
I can tell you I was scared when,
as if by magic,
a series of muddy footprints
appeared on the new white carpet.
I was being good
(honest)
but I think the house is haunted so,
knowing you're going to have a fit,
I've gone over to Gran's for a bit.

BRIAN PATTEN

Black Day

A skelp frae his teacher
For a' he cudna spell:
A skelp frae his mither
For cowpin owre the kail.

A skelp frae his brither
For clourin his braw bat:
And a skelp frae his faither
For the Lord kens what.

WILLIAM SOUTAR

The Sea-Shell

Listen! for a lost world maunners here
Frae the cauld mou o' a shell;
And sae far awa the blufferts blare
And the sea-birds skreel:

And the wail o' women alang yon shore
Whaur the swaw comes rowin in;
And the swurly waters whummlin owre
The cry o' the sailor-men.

WILLIAM SOUTAR

It Was Long Ago

I'll tell you, shall I, something I remember?
Something that still means a great deal to me.
It was long ago.

A dusty road in summer I remember,
A mountain, and an old house, and a tree
That stood, you know,

Behind the house. An old woman I remember
In a red shawl with a grey cat on her knee
Humming under a tree.

She seemed the oldest thing I can remember,
But then perhaps I was not more than three.
It was long ago.

I dragged on the dusty road, and I remember
How the old woman looked over the fence at me
And seemed to know

How it felt to be three, and called out, I remember
'Do you like bilberries and cream for tea?'
I went under the tree

And while she hummed, and the cat purred, I remember
How she filled a saucer with berries and cream for me
So long ago,

Such berries and such cream as I remember
I never had seen before, and never see
To-day, you know.

And that is almost all I can remember,
The house, the mountain, the grey cat on her knee,
Her red shawl, and the tree,

And the taste of the berries, the feel of the sun I remember,
And the smell of everything that used to be
So long ago,

Till the heat on the road outside again I remember,
And how the long dusty road seemed to have for me
No end, you know.

That is the farthest thing I can remember.
It won't mean much to you. It does to me.
Then I grew up, you see.

ELEANOR FARJEON

Blind Man's Bluff

Blindman! Blindman! Blundering about,
Barging round the furniture with hands stretched out.
Bind his eyes and blind his eyes with thick dark stuff,
Mind you see the handkerchief is tied tight enough!

Buffet the old buffer! Biff him in the back!
Tug him by the coat-tails, turn him off his track,
Twist and tease and tickle him, tweak him by the cuff,
Baffle the old buffer in Blind Man's Buff!

Ha, ha, Blindman! snatching at the air!
Ho, ho, Blindman! catching at a chair!
He, he, Blindman! clutching at *me* –
Ha, ha! ho, ho! he, he, he!

    Bustle him and hustle him,
    Muddle and befuddle him,
Bang him off his balance – don't be a funk!
    Banter him! befoozle him!
    Bewilder him! bamboozle him!
Batter, bait, and badger him, and then do a bunk!

Blindman! Blindman! See how he spins!
Bumping and stumping and barking of his shins!
Rumple him and crumple him, treat the buffer rough –
But beware if he should bag you in Blind Man's Buff!

ELEANOR FARJEON

Waiting at the Window

These are my two drops of rain
Waiting on the window-pane.

I am waiting here to see
Which the winning one will be.

Both of them have different names.
One is John and one is James.

All the best and all the worst
Comes from which of them is first.

James has just begun to ooze.
He's the one I want to lose.

John is waiting to begin.
He's the one I want to win.

James is going slowly on.
Something sort of sticks to John.

John is moving off at last.
James is going pretty fast.

John is rushing down the pane.
James is going slow again.

James has met a sort of smear.
John is getting very near.

Is he going fast enough?
(James has found a piece of fluff.)

John has hurried quickly by.
(James was talking to a fly.)

John is there, and John has won!
Look! I told you! Here's the sun!

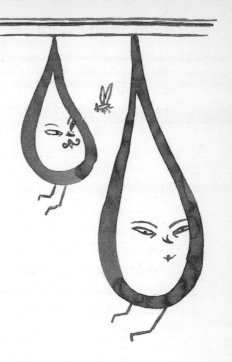

A. A. MILNE

[241]

Paper Boats

Day by day I float my paper boats one by one down the running
stream.
In big black letters I write my name on them and the name of the
village where I live.
I hope that someone in some strange land will find them and
know who I am.
I load my little boats with shiuli flowers from our garden, and
hope that these blooms of the dawn will be carried safely to
land in the night.
I launch my paper boats and look into the sky and see the little
clouds setting their white bulging sails.
I know not what playmate of mine in the sky sends them down
the air to race with my boats!
When night comes I bury my face in my arms and dream that
my paper boats float on and on under the midnight stars.
The fairies of sleep are sailing in them, and the lading is their
baskets full of dreams.

RABINDRANATH TAGORE

Armies in the Fire

The lamps now glitter down the street;
Faintly sound the falling feet;
And the blue even slowly falls
About the garden trees and walls.

Now in the falling of the gloom
The red fire paints the empty room:
And warmly on the roof it looks,
And flickers on the backs of books.

Armies march by tower and spire
Of cities blazing, in the fire; –
Till as I gaze with staring eyes,
The armies fade, the lustre dies.

Then once again the glow returns;
Again the phantom city burns;
And down the red-hot valley, lo!
The phantom armies marching go!

Blinking embers, tell me true
Where are those armies marching to,
And what the burning city is
That crumbles in your furnaces!

ROBERT LOUIS STEVENSON

The Secret Brother

Jack lived in the green-house
When I was six,

With glass and with tomato plants,
Not with slates and bricks.

I didn't have a brother,
Jack became mine.
Nobody could see him,
He never gave a sign.

Just beyond the rockery,
By the apple-tree,
Jack and his old mother lived,
Only for me.

With a tin telephone
Held beneath the sheet,
I would talk to Jack each night.
We would never meet.

Once my sister caught me,
Said, 'He isn't there.
Down among the flower-pots
Cramm the gardener

Is the only person.'
I said nothing, but
Let her go on talking.
Yet I moved Jack out.

He and his old mother
Did a midnight flit.
No one knew his number:
I had altered it.

Only I could see
The sagging washing-line

And my brother making
Our own secret sign.

ELIZABETH JENNINGS

A Boy

Half a mile from the sea,
in a house with a dozen bedrooms
he grew up. Who was he?
Oh, nobody much. A boy
with the usual likes
and more than a few dislikes.
Did he swim much? Nah,
that sea was the Atlantic
and out there is *Iceland*.
He kept his play inland
on an L-shaped football pitch
between the garage and the gate.
What did he eat?
Stuff his grandfather made,
home-made sausages,
potted pig's head.
He got the library keys
and carried eight books at a time
home, and he read.
He read so much
he stayed in the book's world.
Wind rattled the window
of his third-storey room,
but his bed was warm.
And he stayed in his bed

half the day if he could,
reading by candlelight
when the storms struck
and the electricity died.
How do I know all this?
You'd guess how if you tried.

MATTHEW SWEENEY

Bits of Early Days

Still a shock to remember
facing that attacking
dog's fangs and eyes at its gate.
Seeing our slug-eating dog come in
the house, mouth gummed up, plastered.

Still a joy to remember
standing at our palm-fringed beach
watching sunrise streak the sea.
Finding a hen's nest in high grass
full of eggs.
Galloping a horse barebacked
over the village pasture.

Still a shock to remember
eating with fingers and caught
oily handed by my teacher.
Seeing a dog like a goat-hide flattened
there in the road.

Still a joy to remember
myself a small boy milking a cow
in new sunlight.

Smelling asafoetida on
a village baby I held.
Sucking fresh honey from its comb
just robbed.

Still a shock to remember
watching weighted kittens tossed in
the sea's white breakers.
Seeing our village stream dried up
with rocks exposed
like dry guts and brains.

Still a joy to remember
walking barefoot on a bed of dry leaves
there in deep woods.
Finding my goat with all of three
new wobbly kids.

Still a shock to remember
facing that youth-gang attack and all
the needless abuse.
Holding my first identity card
stamped 'Negro'.

Still a joy to remember
walking fourteen miles from four a.m.
into town market.
Surrounded by sounds of church-bell
in sunlight and birdsong.

    JAMES BERRY

The Railway Children

When we climbed the slopes of the cutting
We were eye-level with the white cups
Of the telegraph poles and the sizzling wires.

Like lovely freehand they curved for miles
East and miles west beyond us, sagging
Under their burden of swallows.

We were small and thought we knew nothing
Worth knowing. We thought words travelled the wires
In the shiny pouches of raindrops,

Each one seeded full with the light
Of the sky, the gleam of the lines, and ourselves
So infinitesimally scaled

We could stream through the eye of a needle.

SEAMUS HEANEY

Holly

It rained when it should have snowed.
When we went to gather holly

the ditches were swimming, we were wet
to the knees, our hands were all jags

and water ran up our sleeves.
There should have been berries

but the sprigs we brought into the house
gleamed like smashed bottle-glass.

Now here I am, in a room that is decked
with the red-berried, waxy-leafed stuff,

and I almost forget what it's like
to be wet to the skin or longing for snow.

I reach for a book like a doubter
and want it to flare round my hand,

a black-letter bush, a glittering shield-wall
cutting as holly and ice.

SEAMUS HEANEY

On the Frozen Lake

And in the frosty season, when the sun
Was set, and, visible for many a mile
The cottage-windows through the twilight blaz'd,
I heeded not the summons: – happy time
It was, indeed, for all of us; to me
It was a time of rapture: clear, and loud
The village clock toll'd six; I wheel'd about,
Proud and exulting, like an untired horse,
That cares not for his home. – All shod with steel,
We hiss'd along the polish'd ice, in games
Confederate, imitative of the chace
And woodland pleasures, the resounding horn,
The Pack loud bellowing, and the hunted hare.
So through the darkness and the cold we flew,
And not a voice was idle; with the din,
Meanwhile, the precipices rang aloud,
The leafless trees, and every icy crag
Tinkled like iron, while the distant hills

Into the tumult sent an alien sound
Of melancholy, not unnoticed, while the stars,
Eastward, were sparkling clear, and in the west
The orange sky of evening died away.
    Not seldom from the uproar I retired
Into a silent bay, or sportively
Glanced sideway, leaving the tumultuous throng,
To cut across the image of a star
That gleam'd upon the ice: and oftentimes
When we had given our bodies to the wind,
And all the shadowy banks, on either side,
Came sweeping through the darkness, spinning still
The rapid line of motion; then at once
Have I, reclining back upon my heels,
Stopp'd short; yet still the solitary Cliffs,
Wheeled by me, even as if the earth had roll'd
With visible motion her diurnal round;
Behind me did they stretch in solemn train
Feebler and feebler, and I stood and watch'd
Till all was tranquil as a dreamless sleep.

WILLIAM WORDSWORTH

Meet-on-the-Road

'Now, pray, where are you going?' said Meet-on-the-Road.
'To school, sir, to school, sir,' said Child-as-it-Stood.

'What have you in your basket, child?' said Meet-on-the-Road.
'My dinner, sir, my dinner, sir,' said Child-as-it-Stood.

'What have you for dinner, child?' said Meet-on-the-Road.
'Some pudding, sir, some pudding, sir,' said Child-as-it-Stood.

'Oh, then, I pray, give me a share,' said Meet-on-the-Road.
'I've little enough for myself, sir,' said Child-as-it-Stood.

'What have you got that cloak on for?' said Meet-on-the-Road.
'To keep the wind and cold from me,' said Child-as-it-Stood.

'I wish the wind would blow through you,' said Meet-on-the-
    Road.
'Oh, what a wish! What a wish!' said Child-as-it-Stood.

'Pray, what are those bells ringing for?' said Meet-on-the-Road.
'To ring bad spirits home again,' said Child-as-it-Stood.

'Oh, then I must be going, child!' said Meet-on-the-Road.
'So fare you well, so fare you well,' said Child-as-it-Stood.

ANONYMOUS

Timothy Winters

Timothy Winters comes to school
With eyes as wide as a football pool,
Ears like bombs and teeth like splinters·
A blitz of a boy is Timothy Winters.

His belly is white, his neck is dark,
And his hair is an exclamation mark.
His clothes are enough to scare a crow
And through his britches the blue winds blow.

When teacher talks he won't hear a word
And he shoots down dead the arithmetic-bird,
He licks the patterns off his plate
And he's not even heard of the Welfare State.

Timothy Winters has bloody feet
And he lives in a house on Suez Street,
He sleeps in a sack on the kitchen floor
And they say there aren't boys like him any more.

CHARLES CAUSLEY

'Out, Out –'

The buzz-saw snarled and rattled in the yard
And made dust and dropped stove-length sticks of wood,
Sweet-scented stuff when the breeze drew across it.
And from there those that lifted eyes could count
Five mountain ranges one behind the other
Under the sunset far into Vermont.
And the saw snarled and rattled, snarled and rattled,
As it ran light, or had to bear a load.
And nothing happened: day was all but done.
Call it a day, I wish they might have said
To please the boy by giving him the half hour
That a boy counts so much when saved from work.
His sister stood beside them in her apron
To tell them 'Supper'. At the word, the saw,
As if to prove saws knew what supper meant,
Leaped out at the boy's hand, or seemed to leap –
He must have given the hand. However it was,
Neither refused the meeting. But the hand!
The boy's first outcry was a rueful laugh.
As he swung toward them holding up the hand
Half in appeal, but half as if to keep
The life from spilling. Then the boy saw all –
Since he was old enough to know, big boy

Doing a man's work, though a child at heart –
He saw all spoiled. 'Don't let him cut my hand off –
The doctor, when he comes. Don't let him, sister!'
So. But the hand was gone already.
The doctor put him in the dark of ether.
He lay and puffed his lips out with his breath.
And then – the watcher at his pulse took fright.
No one believed. They listened at his heart.
Little – less – nothing! – and that ended it.
No more to build on there. And they, since they
Were not the one dead, turned to their affairs.

ROBERT FROST

Whirlpool

I saw two hands in the whirlpool
clutching at air,
but when I knelt by the swirling edge
nothing was there.
Behind me, twelve tall green-black trees shook
and scattered their rooks.
I turned to the spinning waters again
and looked.

I saw two legs in the whirlpool
dancing deep.
I see that horrible choreography still
in my turning sleep.
Then I heard the dog from Field o' Blood Farm
howl on its chain;
and gargling out from the whirlpool came the watery sound
of a name.

[253]

I bent my head to the whirlpool,
I saw a face.
Then I knew that I should run for my life
away from that place.
But my eyes and mouth were opening wide, far below
as I drowned.
And the words I tell were silver fish
the day I was found.

CAROL ANN DUFFY

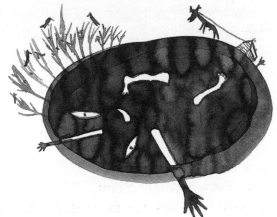

Fairy Story

I went into the wood one day
And there I walked and lost my way

When it was so dark I could not see
A little creature came to me

He said if I would sing a song
The time would not be very long

But first I must let him hold my hand tight
Or else the wood would give me a fright

I sang a song, he let me go
But now I am home again there is nobody I know.

STEVIE SMITH

'Soldier, soldier, won't you marry me?'

Soldier, soldier, won't you marry me?
  It's O the fife and the drum!
How can I marry such a pretty girl as you
  When I've got no hat to put on!

Off to the tailor's she did go
  As fast as she could run,
Brought him back the finest that was there:
  Now, soldier, put it on!

Soldier, soldier, won't you marry me?
  It's O the fife and the drum!
How can I marry such a pretty girl as you
  When I've got no coat to put on!

Back to the tailor's she did go
  As fast as she could run,
Brought him back the finest that was there:
  Now, soldier, put it on!

Soldier, soldier, won't you marry me?
  It's O the fife and the drum!
How can I marry such a pretty girl as you
  When I've got no shoes to put on!

Off to the shoe-shop she did go
  As fast as she could run,
Brought him back the finest that were there:
  Now, soldier, put them on!

Soldier, soldier, won't you marry me?
  It's O the fife and the drum!
How can I marry such a pretty girl as you
  When I've a wife and babies at home!

ANONYMOUS

[255]

'Piping down the valleys wild'

Piping down the valleys wild,
Piping songs of pleasant glee,
On a cloud I saw a child,
And he laughing said to me:

'Pipe a song about a Lamb!'
So I piped with merry chear.
'Piper, pipe that song again;'
So I piped: he wept to hear.

'Drop thy pipe, thy happy pipe;
'Sing thy songs of happy chear:'
So I sung the same again,
While he wept with joy to hear.

'Piper, sit thee down and write
'In a book, that all may read.'
So he vanish'd from my sight,
And I pluck'd a hollow reed,

And I made a rural pen,
And I stain'd the water clear,
And I wrote my happy songs
Every child may joy to hear.

WILLIAM BLAKE

Child's Song

My cheap toy lamp
gives little light
all night, all night,
when my muscles cramp.

Sometimes I touch your hand
across my cot,
and our fingers knot,
but there's no hand

to take me home –
no Caribbean
island, where even
the shark is at home.

It must be heaven.
There on that island
the white sand shines
like a birchwood fire.

Help! Saw me in two,
put me on the shelf!
Sometimes the little muddler
can't stand himself!

    ROBERT LOWELL.

Brendon Gallacher
for my brother Maxie

He was seven and I was six, my Brendon Gallacher.
He was Irish and I was Scottish, my Brendon Gallacher.
His father was in prison; he was a cat burglar.

My father was a communist party full-time worker.
He had six brothers and I had one, my Brendon Gallacher.

He would hold my hand and take me by the river
Where we'd talk all about his family being poor.
He'd get his mum out of Glasgow when he got older.
A wee holiday someplace nice. Some place far.
I'd tell my mum about my Brendon Gallacher

How his mum drank and his daddy was a cat burglar.
And she'd say, 'why not have him round to dinner?'
No, no, I'd say he's got big holes in his trousers.
I like meeting him by the burn in the open air.
Then one day after we'd been friends two years,

One day when it was pouring and I was indoors,
My mum says to me, 'I was talking to Mrs Moir
Who lives next door to your Brendon Gallacher
Didn't you say his address was 24 Novar?
She says there are no Gallachers at 24 Novar

There never have been any Gallachers next door.'
And he died then, my Brendon Gallacher,
Flat out on my bedroom floor, his spiky hair,
His impish grin, his funny flapping ear.
Oh Brendon. Oh my Brendon Gallacher.

JACKIE KAY

The Way Through the Woods

They shut the road through the woods
Seventy years ago.
Weather and rain have undone it again,
And now you would never know

There was once a road through the woods
Before they planted the trees.
It is underneath the coppice and heath
And the thin anemones.
Only the keeper sees
That, where the ring-dove broods,
And the badgers roll at ease,
There was once a road through the woods.

Yet, if you enter the woods
Of a summer evening late,
When the night-air cools on the trout-ringed pools
Where the otter whistles his mate,
(They fear not men in the woods,
Because they see so few.)
You will hear the beat of a horse's feet,
And the swish of a skirt in the dew,
Steadily cantering through
The misty solitudes,
As though they perfectly knew
The old lost road through the woods . . .
But there is no road through the woods.

RUDYARD KIPLING

Castaway

I have no name for today
But itself. Long ago
I lost count of the days.
Castaways have no mirror
But the sea, that leaves its wrinkles
On themselves, too. Every morning

I see how the sun comes up
Unpublicised; there is no news
On this beach. What I do
Neither the tall birds on the shore,
Nor the animals in the bush
Care about. They have all time
And no time, each one about
Its business, foraging, breeding.
I thought that they had respect
For a human. Here there are creatures
That jostle me, others that crawl
On my loved flesh. I am the food
They were born for, endlessly shrilling
Their praises. I have seen the bones
In the jungle, that are the cradle
We came from and go back to.

   R. S. THOMAS

The First Music

What was the first music
After the chirping of birds, the barking of foxes,
After the hoot of owls, the mooing of cows,
The murmur of dawn birds, winds in the trees?
Did all these tell the first men they must make
Their own music? Mothers would lullaby
Their babies to sleep, warriors certainly shouted.
But what was the first music that was its own
Purpose, a pattern or phrasing, a quality
Of sound that came between silences and cast out
All other possible sounds? It must have been man

Singing in love and exultation, hearing
The high sweet song of blackbirds. When did he fashion
A harp or horn? O how much I would give
To hear that first and pristine music and know
That it changed the turning planet and visited stars.

ELIZABETH JENNINGS

Phizzog

This face you got,
This here phizzog you carry around,
You never picked it out for yourself
  at all, at all – did you?
This here phizzog – somebody handed it
  to you – am I right?
Somebody said, 'Here's yours, now go see
  what you can do with it.'
Somebody slipped it to you and it was like
  a package marked:
'No goods exchanged after being taken away' –
This face you got.

CARL SANDBURG

Buffalo Dusk

The buffaloes are gone.
And those who saw the buffaloes are gone.
Those who saw the buffaloes by thousands and how they pawed
    the prairie sod into dust with their hoofs, their great heads
    down pawing on in a great pageant of dusk,
Those who saw the buffaloes are gone.
And the buffaloes are gone.

CARL SANDBURG

Poem from a Three-Year-Old

And will the flowers die?

And will the people die?

And every day do you grow old, do I
grow old, no I'm not old, do
flowers grow old?

Old things – do you throw them out?

Do you throw old people out?

And how you know a flower that's old?

The petals fall, the petals fall from flowers,
and do the petals fall from people too,
every day more petals fall until the
floor where I would like to play I
want to play is covered with old
flowers and people all the same
together lying there with petals fallen
on the dirty floor I want to play

the floor you come and sweep
with the huge broom.

The dirt you sweep, what happens that,
what happens all the dirt you sweep
from flowers and people, what
happens all the dirt? Is all the
dirt what's left of flowers and
people, all the dirt there in a
heap under the huge broom that
sweeps everything away? Why you work so hard, why brush
and sweep to make a heap of dirt?

And who will bring new flowers?

And who will bring new people? Who will
bring new flowers to put in water
where no petals fall on to the
floor where I would like to
play? Who will bring new flowers
that will not hang their heads
like tired old people wanting sleep?
Who will bring new flowers that
do not split and shrivel every
day? And if we have new flowers
will we have new people too to
keep the flowers alive and give
them water?

And will the new young flowers die?

And will the new young people die?

And why?

BRENDAN KENNELLY

Sea Wind: A Song
after Rilke

Sea wind, you rise
From the night waves below,
Not that we see you come and go,
But as the blind know things we know
And feel you on our face,
And all you are
Or ever were is space,
Sea wind, come from so far
To fill us with this restlessness
That will outlast your own –
So the fig tree,
When you are gone,
Sea wind, still bends and leans out toward the sea
And goes on blossoming alone.

DONALD JUSTICE

How She Went to Ireland

Dora's gone to Ireland
   Through the sleet and snow;
Promptly she has gone there
   In a ship, although
Why she's gone to Ireland
   Dora does not know.

That was where, yea, Ireland,
   Dora wished to be:
When she felt, in lone times,
   Shoots of misery,
Often there, in Ireland,
   Dora wished to be.

Hence she's gone to Ireland,
   Since she meant to go,
Through the drift and darkness
   Onward labouring, though
That she's gone to Ireland
   Dora does not know.

THOMAS HARDY

Heart Burial

They fetched it along, and they slipped it in,
Mr Hardy's heart in a biscuit tin.

Mrs Hardy said, This grave is my bed
And my husband Thomas was not well-bred.

And the heart spoke up, and it mildly said,
Give me to my old dog Wessex instead,

Give me to my surly dog Wessex instead,
But Wessex was busy with a fresh sheep's head,

And the rector pretended he did not hear,
And dry was the sexton and needed beer,

And bumpetty bump and din din din
Earth fell on the box and the biscuit tin.

GEOFFREY GRIGSON

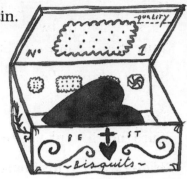

Brian O Linn

Brian O Linn had no breeches to wear,
He got an old sheepskin to make him a pair,
With the fleshy side out and the woolly side in,
'They'll be pleasant and cool', says Brian O Linn.

Brian O Linn had no shirt to his back,
He went to a neighbour's, and borrowed a sack,
Then he puckered the meal bag in under his chin,
'Sure they'll take them for ruffles,' says Brian O Linn.

Brian O Linn was hard up for a coat,
So he borrowed the skin of a neighbouring goat,
With the horns sticking out from his oxters, and then,
'Sure they'll take them for pistols,' says Brian O Linn.

Brian O Linn had no hat to put on,
So he got an old beaver to make him a one,
There was none of the crown left and less of the brim,
'Sure there's fine ventilation,' says Brian O Linn.

Brian O Linn had no brogues for his toes,
He hopped in two crab-shells to serve him for those.
Then he split up two oysters that match'd like a twin,
'Sure they'll shine out like buckles,' says Brian O Linn.

Brian O Linn had no watch to put on,
So he scooped out a turnip to make him a one.
Then he placed a young cricket in-under the skin,
'Sure they'll think it is ticking,' says Brian O Linn.

Brian O Linn to his house had no door,
He'd the sky for a roof, and the bog for a floor;
He'd a way to jump out, and a way to swim in,
''Tis a fine habitation,' says Brian O Linn.

Brian O Linn went a-courting one night,
He set both the mother and daughter to fight;
To fight for his hand they both stripped to the skin,
'Sure! I'll marry you both,' says Brian O Linn.

Brian O Linn, his wife and wife's mother,
They all lay down in the bed together,
The sheets they were old and the blankets were thin,
'Lie close to the wall,' says Brian O Linn.

Brian O Linn, his wife and wife's mother,
Were all going home o'er the bridge together,
The bridge it broke down, and they all tumbled in,
'We'll go home by the water,' says Brian O Linn.

ANONYMOUS

Fairy Tale

He built himself a house,
        his foundations,
        his stones,
        his walls,
        his roof overhead,
        his chimney and smoke,
        his view from the window.

He made himself a garden,
        his fence
        his thyme
        his earthworm
        his evening dew.

He cut out his bit of sky above.

And he wrapped the garden in the sky
and the house in the garden
and packed the lot in a handkerchief
and went off
lone as an Arctic fox
through the cold
unending
rain
into the world.

MIROSLAV HOLUB
(translated by
George Theiner)

A Tent

A tent went up on the grass:
    just room for a boy and his brother,
who waited for day to pass
kept wishing that day would pass
    as they'd never wished of another.

At last they got their wish.
    Darkness fell and off they went
feeling quite daredevilish –
yes, really daredevilish –
    to spend a night in that tent.

Night is dizzy and deep;
    the wall of a tent is thin;
they were almost too scared to sleep,
but whispered each other to sleep
    as stars and ghosts listened in.

And the tent flew through the night
    on the back of the turning world,
which brought them home all right,
them and the tent, still upright
    and now lavishly dew-pearled.

    CHRISTOPHER REID

My Papa's Waltz

The whiskey on your breath
Could make a small boy dizzy;
But I hung on like death:
Such waltzing was not easy.

We romped until the pans
Slid from the kitchen shelf;
My mother's countenance
Could not unfrown itself.

The hand that held my wrist
Was battered on one knuckle;
At every step you missed
My right ear scraped a buckle.

You beat time on my head
With a palm caked hard by dirt,
Then waltzed me off to bed
Still clinging to your shirt.

THEODORE ROETHKE

Back in the Playground Blues

I dreamed I was back in the playground, I was about four feet
   high
Yes dreamed I was back in the playground, standing about four
   feet high
Well the playground was three miles long and the playground
   was five miles wide

It was broken black tarmac with a high wire fence all around
Broken black dusty tarmac with a high fence running all around
And it had a special name to it, they called it The Killing Ground

Got a mother and a father, they're one thousand years away
The rulers of The Killing Ground are coming out to play
Everybody thinking: 'Who they going to play with today?'

[270]

Well you get it for being Jewish
And you get it for being black
Get it for being chicken
And you get it for fighting back
You get it for being big and fat
Get it for being small
Oh those who get it get it and get it
For any damn thing at all

Sometimes they take a beetle, tear off its six legs one by one
Beetle on its black back, rocking in the lunchtime sun
But a beetle can't beg for mercy, a beetle's not half the fun

I heard a deep voice talking, it had that iceberg sound
'It prepares them for Life' – but I have never found
Any place in my life worse than The Killing Ground.

ADRIAN MITCHELL

Song of the Galley-Slaves

We pulled for you when the wind was against us and the sails
    were low.
        Will you never let us go?
We ate bread and onions when you took towns, or ran aboard
    quickly when you were beaten back by the foe.
The Captains walked up and down the deck in fair weather
    singing songs, but we were below.
We fainted with our chins on the oars and you did not see that
    we were idle, for we still swung to and fro.
        Will you never let us go?
The salt made the oar-handles like shark-skin; our knees were
    cut to the bone with salt-cracks; our hair was stuck to our
    foreheads; and our lips were cut to the gums, and you

whipped us because we could not row.
     Will you never let us go?
But, in a little time, we shall run out of the port-holes as the
    water runs along the oar-blade, and though you tell the
    others to row after us you will never catch us till you catch the
    oar-thresh and tie up the winds in the belly of the sail. Aho!
     Will you never let us go?

RUDYARD KIPLING

The Arrest of Oscar Wilde at the Cadogan Hotel

He sipped at a weak hock and seltzer
    As he gazed at the London skies
Through the Nottingham lace of the curtains
    Or was it his bees-winged eyes?

To the right and before him Pont Street
    Did tower in her new built red,
As hard as the morning gaslight
    That shone on his unmade bed.

'I want some more hock in my seltzer,
    And Robbie, please give me your hand –
Is this the end or beginning?
    How can I understand?

'So you've brought me the latest *Yellow Book*:
    And Buchan has got in it now:
Approval of what is approved of
    Is as false as a well-kept vow.

'More hock, Robbie – where is the seltzer?
    Dear boy, pull again at the bell!

They are all little better than *cretins*,
    Though this *is* the Cadogan Hotel.

'One astrakhan coat is at Willis's –
    Another one's at the Savoy:
Do fetch my morocco portmanteau,
    And bring them on later, dear boy.'

A thump, and a murmur of voices –
    ('Oh why must they make such a din?')
As the door of the bedroom swung open
    And TWO PLAIN CLOTHES POLICEMEN came in:

'Mr Woilde, we 'ave come for tew take yew
    Where felons and criminals dwell:
We must ask yew tew leave with us quoietly
    For this *is* the Cadogan Hotel.'

He rose, and he put down *The Yellow Book*.
    He staggered – and, terrible-eyed,
He brushed past the palms on the staircase
    And was helped to a hansom outside.

JOHN BETJEMAN

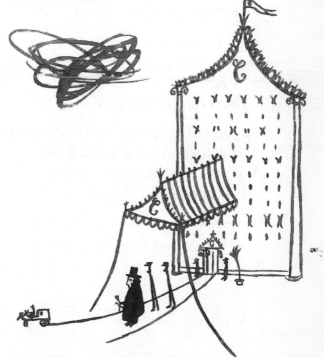

[273]

Acknowledgements

The editor and publishers gratefully acknowledge permission to reprint copyright material in this book as follows:

JOHN AGARD: 'So-So-Joe' from *No Hickory, No Dickory, No Dock* (Viking Puffin, 1996), reprinted by permission of Caroline Sheldon Literary Agency on behalf of the author. SIMON ARMITAGE: 'Ten Pence Story' from *Zoom*, published by Bloodaxe Books Ltd, 1989, reprinted by permission of the publisher. W. H. AUDEN: 'The Ballad of Baranaby', 'O What is that Sound', 'Twelve Songs XI' from *Collected Poems*, 'Choruses & Songs II' from *The English Auden*, reprinted by permission of Faber and Faber Ltd. GEORGE BARKER: 'What Does the Clock Say' from *Dibby Dubby Dhu*, 'The Call to One Another' from *To Aylsham Fair*, reprinted by permission of Faber and Faber Ltd. HILAIRE BELLOC: 'Goldophin Horne' from *Cautionary Verses* by Hilaire Belloc, published by Random House (Red Fox), reprinted by permission of Peters Fraser & Dunlop Group Ltd on behalf of The Estate of Hillaire Belloc. JOHN BETJEMAN: 'The Arrest of Oscar Wilde at the Cadogan Hotel' and 'Death in Leamington' from *Collected Poems*, published by John Murray (Publishers) Ltd, reprinted by permission of the publisher. ELIZABETH BISHOP: 'Manners' from *The Complete Poems 1927–79*, reprinted by permission of Farrar, Straus and Giroux, LLC. GEORGE MACKAY BROWN, 'A Boy in a Snow Shower' and 'Following a Lark: A Country Boy Goes to School' from *Following a Lark*, 'Beachcomber' from *Fishermen With Ploughs*, published by John Murray (Publishers) Ltd, 1996, reprinted by permission of the publisher. CHARLES CAUSLEY: 'What has happened to Lulu?', 'The Green Man in the Garden', 'Ballad of the Bread Man', 'I Saw a Jolly Hunter', 'Tom Bone', 'Timothy Winters' from *Collected Poems 1951–2000*, published by Macmillan, reprinted by permission of David Higham Associates Ltd. E. E. CUMMINGS: 'hist whist' and 'why did you go' from *Complete Poems 1904–1962* by E. E. Cummings, edited by George J. Firmage, by permission of W. W. Norton & Company, copyright © 1991 by the Trustees for the E. E. Cummings Trust and George James Firmage. CAROL ANN DUFFY: 'Poker', 'Queens' and 'Whirlpool' from *Meeting Midnight*, reprinted by permission of Faber and Faber Ltd; 'The Legend' from *The Other Country*, published by Anvil Press Poetry, 1990, reprinted by permission of the publisher. RICHARD EDWARDS: 'Lower the Diver' and 'A Crime to Report' reprinted by permission of the author. T. S. ELIOT: 'The Song of Jellicles' and 'Old Deuteronomy' from *Old Possum's Book of Practical Cats*, reprinted by permission of Faber and Faber Ltd. ELEANOR FARJEON: 'In Goes Robin' from *Silver Sand and Snow*, published by Michael Joseph; 'Wheelbarrow' and 'It Was Long Ago' from *Blackbird Has Spoken*, published by Macmillan; 'Blind Man's Buff' from *Then There Were Three*, published by Michael Joseph, reprinted by permission of

Index of Poets